FAMILY REVISION

ANCIENT WISDOM TO HEAL THE MODERN FAMILY

BY JEREMY PRYOR
FOREWORD BY JEFFERSON BETHKE

DEDICATION

To April, my team building life partner.

So much of what it has taken me years to figure out with my head you knew first in your heart.

I'm overwhelmed with gratitude for the gift of you.

TABLE OF CONTENTS

Dedication   iii

Acknowledgments   v

Foreword   vii

Introduction   1

How Family has Changed   12

How to Build a Family Team   41

Tool #1 - The Value of Family   45

Tool #2 - The Scope of Family   63

Tool #3 - The Mission of the Family   78

Tool #4 - The Roles of the Family   98

Tool #5 - The Training of the Family   120

Tool #6 - The Resources of the Family   137

Tool #7 - The Rhythms of the Family   162

Conclusion: God's Kingdom as a Family of Families   181

Epilogue by April Pryor   183

ACKNOWLEDGMENTS

First, I'd like to thank the upstream relationships that have faithfully and skillfully helped me construct my father's compass.

- My Dad, Jerry Pryor: Your steadfast faithfulness has been like a beacon in my life, always guiding me to the Scriptures and our Heavenly Father.
- My Father-in-Law, Donald Seely: Your stories, your encouragement and the example you've set in the way you raised your daughter have guided me in ways you'll never know. We miss you and look forward to that largest of family reunions in our Father's Kingdom.
- My prayer warrior friend, David Sheldon: Your prayer over me is what finally released the writer in me.
- My father-coach, Mark Whitmore: The time, dedication, and love you showed to me by saying the necessary and hard things have healed both me and multiple relationships within my family. I'm so grateful for you!
- Next, there are the horizontal relationships who have influenced and inspired my insights on fatherhood.
- My business/ministry partner and brother-in-Christ, Stephen Mowry: You've stuck by me through 20 years of seeking the Kingdom in so many diverse areas. Your loyal love for me has been a ballast and our deep conversations have helped me go so much deeper into these truths.
- My philosopher friend, Gavin Long: You always manage to make my vision of our Father's Kingdom bigger than I imagined.

- Our family teams partners, Jefferson and Alyssa Bethke: I'm so grateful for the miraculous way our Father drew us together. You make this work a joy everyday and we love you all!
- My constant encourager, Blake Smith: You always believed and boldly told me that I have something to say.
- My friends who gave me feedback: Matt Chandler, Jason Diffner and Tim Schmoyer.
- My book editor, Adam Palmer: Man, did I ever need your help!

Finally I just want to thank my amazing kids, Kelsey, Jackson, Sydney, Elisa and Kaira. It's the greatest privilege of my life to get be your father and to get to lead this team. Never stop believing that we're better together.

FOREWORD

I think the day was December 29, 2012.

I was speaking at a conference in Louisville, KY. I had only met Jeremy and his wife, April, once before. When he heard Alyssa and I were down the road from them (they live in Cincinnati area about 90 minutes away), he said we should meet up in the middle and grab breakfast.

That day became the day our marriage and family changed forever.

Not just because we ate at Cracker Barrel! Even though that was undoubtedly a contributing factor (Cracker Barrel and Chick-fil-A are life, and if you don't agree I'm not sure we can be friends).

But seriously, that was the day that began our long and winding journey the past seven years of reimagining and restructuring the vision for our family and our marriage.

Here's the best part. There wasn't anything absolutely crazy I remember Jeremy and April saying that morning at breakfast.

There was just a lot of little fascinating ideas and thoughts coming out in between the lines that intrigued me. I loved what they were talking about, and something in my brain seemed to be captured by it.

So, thanks to the Lord's grace, over the past seven years our family has formed a pretty unique and close relationship with the Pryor's. Even though we've never lived closer than 2,000 miles from each other (now probably 5,000 from Maui to Ohio), we've been lucky enough to leverage our job (which has a high travel rate) to live in their home for a few periods. We also have had them out to Maui and Washington where we lived, and we even stayed with them in their apartment for a few weeks when they lived in Israel.

From Cracker Barrel to all of those moments above, it was really just as simple as us being captured by an idea, and then pursuing it more or going one layer deeper, one small step at a time.

The Pryor's inspired us to build a multi-generational family team on mission.

I remember our first question seven years ago was what? What is that?

Then it was why.
And now I'd say we are in the season of how.

Honestly, I think that's how it goes forever until you die. And that's the fun part. Once you're captured there is always more to lean into and see with fresh eyes from Jesus. He's constantly growing us, molding us, shaping us, and taking us on a journey and there is always enough grace for every step of the way.

The cool part about the book you hold right now is it's a full unleashing of the answers to those questions. It'll answer the what, the why, and the how.

What you're holding is an invaluable resource for your family and one that can change your family's life and trajectory for the better, if you lean into it. Don't be afraid to be captured by the vision. And then realize you have, hopefully, a long life to

take one step at a time towards the goal of building your team
(and one that will continue and build on your faithfulness
and obedience even after you die) under the lordship of Jesus.

Jefferson Bethke

INTRODUC-
TION

The Lord said to Abram, "...All the families on earth will be blessed through you." **Genesis 12:3**

God loves the concept of family. It was his idea. Family is the way he chose to order his world at the dawn of creation, and it's through experiencing family that human beings can begin to grasp the many aspects of God's nature.

But this can create a problem. If God's character is revealed through the picture of a loving family, then to distort or destroy this picture would lead to a distortion of our understanding of God. And that is exactly what is happening in the western world—at an alarming scale.

Sigmund Freud once suggested that no one lost his faith in God without first losing faith in his own father. Counseling rooms are filled with broken people rehashing their childhoods in detail to discover the origins of their issues. We simply cannot escape the link between our experience of family and our connection with the divine.

But why does our culture seem to have an almost universal struggle with building a functional family? What is the root? And why does this problem seem as acute in Christian homes as in non-Christian homes? Does the Bible provide insights that can heal the modern family?

Thankfully, when it comes to family, Scripture provides exactly the model we need, and that's found in the person through whom God promised to "bless all the families on Earth," Abraham.

While Abraham was far from the perfect father, his perspective on family has blessed my family more than I'll ever be able to express. He is the model patriarch and he has demonstrated for me how to build and love my own family. His understanding of fatherhood is the antidote to the disease that has infected the modern family.

So if you're struggling to figure out this messy, maddening, beautiful thing we call family, then consider with me the character of Abraham. Maybe this is the generation when you will receive the blessing through Abraham God promised to your family almost 5,000 years ago.

MY STORY

"Brothers and fathers, listen to me! The God of glory appeared to our father Abraham..." **Acts 7:2**

I grew up in the beautiful Pacific Northwest just outside of Seattle, Washington—a place famous for coffee, rain and dog ownership. In fact, it's the one city in the country where dogs outnumber children, and at one time that made perfect sense to me. It was a time when I felt kids required a lot of work for not much of a reward. As the saying goes, "The more I time I spend with your kids, the more I love my dog."

But from a young age, I also loved the Bible. And because I really wanted to understand the Old Testament, at the age of 23 I headed off to Jerusalem for a semester of studying Hebrew.

Rudyard Kipling once wrote, "What knows he of England who only England knows?" His point being: it's really difficult to understand your culture from the inside. It's only once you really get to know another culture that you can, for the first time, understand what is truly unique about the culture from which you came.

Kipling's observation rang true for me in 1997, when I had

my first immersive, cross-cultural experience in Jerusalem. While I expected to learn more about the Bible during this time, I didn't anticipate how challenged I'd be by my sudden exposure to the diverse cultures in the Middle East. My semester in Jerusalem provided one major epiphany after another about American culture, because now I could begin to see my own culture from an outsider's perspective.

These realizations culminated one day while I was sitting on a bench next to a sidewalk close to the Old City. A group of strollers rolled by, and when I looked up to see who was pushing them, I was surprised to see a group of fathers. In America, a group of strollers is typically comprised of a mommy brigade out for some exercise. So what were these men doing with all of those babies? Throughout my time in Israel I had seen men be unusually interested in their children—at least, it seemed unusual to me—but it wasn't until I saw this scene that the difference became stark enough that I began to ask questions.

If I was honest with myself, at the time I saw kids as more of a woman's thing. The main reason for a guy to have a baby, I thought, was to give into his wife's need to fulfill her maternal instinct, or perhaps to have that experience of being a dad as a part of a fulfilling life.

If you really must have kids, I thought, you should do it at a time and in a way that would be the least disruptive to your preferred lifestyle. So what I saw in Jerusalem was a real mystery to me, and I wanted to understand the difference between the way I thought about children and the way these Jewish men thought about them.

So I began to read and ask questions about where these kid-loving values originated. The answer actually shocked me. I was told it came from the Bible. This did not compute! When I read the Bible I saw Jesus and the Apostles running around the world, mostly as single men, doing ministry; there's precious little time for stroller-pushing when you're reaching the world with the Gospel.

Further, when I tried to understand which part of Bible had most influenced this culture of family, I was told that the answer could be summed up by one person: Abraham. Really? I had always heard of Abraham as a model of faith, but I had never seriously considered Abraham as a model father.

But what I ultimately discovered in the pages of the very Bible I had dedicated the past eight years of my life to study was a view of family that was entirely new to me—and it blew my mind. I discovered that my view of family at the time was the farthest thing from the biblical model of family actually provided to us in Scripture, and that I had been completely immersed in a notion of family that set itself up largely in opposition to God's design.

Why hadn't I seen this before? Christians in the West are largely blind to what the Scriptures say about family because we've accepted the culture's redefinition of the concept. We need to rediscover the original vision for the family: a family revision.

Let's begin with our current reality—the unique way we westerners think about the concept of family.

INTRODUCING THE WESTERN FAMILY

"You should know this, Timothy, that in the last days there will be very difficult times. For people will love only themselves and their money. They will be boastful and proud, scoffing at God,

disobedient to their parents, and ungrateful. They will consider nothing sacred." -2 Timothy 3:1-2

Imagine that someone from the distant past was able to travel to the present and spend a week with your family. What do you think would strike them as strange?

Once they got past the initial shock of cars and airplanes and The Weather Channel, they would probably be struck by how individualistic families had become—how it feels like most people today use the family for their own personal gain. First-generation immigrants to America from much older cultures make a similar observation. Because they've typically made great sacrifices to give their children a better future, they're surprised and confused by the individualism so prevalent within the western family.

In this culture, it's simply understood that each member of the family is into their own thing—the son plays soccer and the daughter dances; Mom's into her weekly book club and Dad loves to golf. This hyper-individualism is at the very core of what it means to be a "good" western family.

At the most fundamental level, the belief underlying this western philosophy is that the family should serve the individual more than the individual should serve the family. More specifically, the typical western family is often comprised of parents who believe their family exists to provide an effective springboard for the present and future success of each individual family member—often within a well-meaning, loving, secure environment.

Sounds pretty good, right? This ideal has become part of our cultural DNA—what could possibly be wrong with it? To understand how this relatively recent shift in our understanding of family might actually be responsible for the messes many families experience today, we need to examine where this philosophy ultimately leads.

Everyone tends to withdraw from the family and it makes less and less sense to make personal sacrifices. The family is not the environment through which you live your life but it's a temporary, disposable environment that is designed to be transcended.

"Thanks for the 18 years of assistance, Mom and Dad, I'll see you at Christmas." Sure, if the relationship is close, we might expect a few calls and emails in between—or maybe even more frequent visits if the kids choose to live in the same general area—but that's pretty much the best-case scenario.

And why shouldn't our kids just move on? What more can we expect? After all, if we've done our jobs as parents, our kids should "leave the nest" and fly while we enjoy our "golden years," right?

Now I'm certainly not saying that kids shouldn't become skilled and empowered individuals. And if the concept of "family" includes only a mother and father plus their children, then the kids will inevitably outgrow that structure as they mature. The notion of a nuclear family consisting only of parents and the kids under their roof is, historically speaking, a recent phenomenon. That is not how Abraham thought about family.

To understand how family was viewed in almost every corner of the world throughout most of human history, we have to look back to what came before.

REINTRODUCING THE CLASSICAL FAMILY

"The Lord forbid that I should give you the inheritance that was passed down by my ancestors." -1 Kings 21:3

In virtually every ancient civilization—and throughout all of history, until very recent times—a similar philosophy of family existed. We'll call this the Classical Philosophy of Family.

The three basic tenets of this philosophy might seem strange or foreign to most western families today:

1. Individual success is dependent on valuing the family team over the individual.
2. Family success is determined multigenerationally.
3. The primary task of the current generation is to faithfully steward, expand and pass on the resources of the family to the next generation.

So where did this philosophy originate and why was it so pervasive? Did delegates from every part of the world come together and agree that this philosophy was superior to all other options for the family? On the contrary, this philosophy emerged naturally, independently and repeatedly all around the world, in every kind of civilization. In fact, it required some relatively new philosophical ideas and a very unusual set of circumstances for modern westerners to believe anything different from this classical understanding of family. Why is that?

First, consider the natural life cycle of a human being. Each of us is born helpless and, should we live into old age, dies helpless. If someone hadn't decided to sacrifice themselves in order to care for us, we wouldn't be alive. And in fact, in most societies, the very person who provided this care for so many years receives that same level of sacrifice and love from us as they grow old. Without this cycle of care, few humans would survive their own childhood. Only in very recent times has the state been wealthy enough to provide services to protect and provide care for children and elderly people when the family is unwilling or unable.

Next, consider the natural dangers in the world. If families didn't come together to support and protect one another in deeply sacrificial and interdependent ways, they would be wiped out by sickness, bandits, famine and other largely unpredictable disasters. Growing up with an expectation of relative peace and prosperity throughout one's entire life is only a very recent phenomenon.

Also consider that at one time your social standing and prospects in life would have depended largely on the material things your parents and grandparents passed down to you. Imagine if your home, land and comfortable quality of life were not just a given but were inherited through eight generations of grueling, selfless sacrifice. If these stories of sacrifice were passed down to you along with these valuable assets—and you knew that your children and grandchildren's quality of life depended almost entirely on how you stewarded what was given to you by your parents—then "family" might mean something very different to you and to your children.

Our cultural perception is that modern society has made great strides toward a meritocracy, in which each individual can earn the success and prosperity they experience—regardless of the family into which they were born. However, this goal has required an enormous amount of social engineering from a powerful and wealthy centralized government, which was virtually impossible until very recent times—and even then, we're still a long ways away from achieving a true meritocracy.

In summary, a classical family was forced to work very closely together, and the fate of the individual was so closely tied to the strength and success of the family that the best thing anyone could do was to serve one's family for life. But much has changed.

The western and classical philosophies of family are radically different. Do you identify more with one philosophy than the other? Which one do you think is right? When God designed the family, did he have one of these two views in mind?

WHAT DOES THE BIBLE SAY?

"This is what the LORD says: "Stand at the crossroads and look; ask for the ancient paths, ask where the good way is and walk in it, and you will find rest for your souls." -Jeremiah 6:16

We all tend to assume we know what a family is. Afterall, everyone has decades of experience in the subject of family. We all have extensive experience in our families of origin and most of you reading this are building families. But what if we don't know what a family is? What if we don't know what a family was actually designed to be? What if we lost the blueprint for family and we're building something else? What if each of us needs to decide what paradigm of family we believe is most consistent with what God lays out in Scripture?

In order to answer the question of which philosophy of family is more biblical, we must turn to the Bible itself to discover God's design for the family. After all, family was His idea. And if the Bible reveals to us God's design for the family, all believers must start from that design. Once we begin to unpack the biblical blueprint for family, it will be clear to see that this design is totally incompatible with its modern, western counterpart.

Perhaps the simplest way to summarize the Bible's position on family is to say that the Bible—in both the Old and New Testaments—presents a redeemed form of the classical philosophy of family. And although the principles of God's Word can critique and correct any modern idea, the western philosophy of family did not exist in biblical times the way it does today, so the authors of the Bible were not specifically making a case for or against it.

Which means that you and I have a serious problem on our hands. Adopting a philosophy of family different from what you've probably experienced and your culture promotes is an extremely difficult thing to do, like trying to swim upstream in a rushing river. You have to be equipped. It requires deep understanding, powerful tools and plenty of training to begin to live with a biblical family philosophy.

That's why I wrote this book. The rest of this blueprint will examine the biblical model of family and provide resources to parents wanting to grow in their understanding and application of God's design for the family.

HOW FAMILY HAS CHANGED

Often when I discuss these contrasting views of family and encourage others to begin to make a change, it can feel like I'm asking them to paint a picture of something they've never seen. What did a classical family look like in ancient times? So as we dive into the scriptural view of family, I'd like to demonstrate the contrast by introducing you to two twelve-year-old boys. I've written these two fictitious interviews to explore how different these ideas are especially as they are experienced by children. We'll begin with a first century boy named Yitzach.

YITZACH SON OF ASA AND BRAD JOHNSON

"The father of a righteous child has great joy; a man who fathers a wise son rejoices in him." **Proverbs 23:24**

Yitzach's bio: Yitzach lives in the village of Tekoa, south of Jerusalem. He has six siblings: three older brothers, two older sisters, and one younger sister. His family owns 23 acres of olive trees and 35 acres of land planted with wheat, as well as 84 sheep and 14 goats. They own a family home in the village, as well as a variety of sheds on their land. They employ three full-time servants, two of whom assist with the household and one who is an assistant foreman for projects. They employ anywhere between two and 20 seasonal employees, depending on harvest time and other peak seasons.

All of Yitzach's siblings live in his family home, including his older brother's wife and their two children, his great aunt, and his grandfather, who is a widower and a village elder representing their family and serving their community.

Yitzach, please describe your family: We are descendants of

Abraham, Isaac and Jacob, from the tribe of Judah and the line of Jahab, who led our family in the war against the Greeks 200 years ago. Before the Romans took over, our family owned 200 acres of olive trees, but we have slowly begun to sell our land to pay the heavy taxes put on us by the Romans. My father has asked me to learn a new trade for our family in case we lose the rest of our land.

Who are your heroes? My biggest hero is Jahab. We still have his sword and shield hanging in our home, and my grandfather tells us stories about him and other ancestors of our clan every Sabbath.

What do you want to do when you get older? I'm hoping to learn the skill of blacksmithing and to sell my wares and services to help my family keep our land—and eventually to buy more of it back from a Roman centurion.

What is your family hoping to accomplish this year? We are hoping to save enough from the harvest and from all the lambs that were born this year to buy back one of our acres, and to add on a room to the house for when my second-oldest brother is wed.

What would you like to accomplish this year? I'm learning ancient Hebrew from our Rabbi and hope to honor my family by being able to read the Torah well at my Bar mitzvah. My parents are also paying for me to learn some valuable skills from Joseph the blacksmith, and I hope to bring in twice as much this year as last year by repairing equipment for families in our village.

What is your biggest hope? That the Messiah would return and bring justice for my family for all the suffering we endured under the Romans. I also hope that our home and land would be established forever and that our descendants will live in peace in the land.

What is your biggest fear? That we would be forced to pay even higher taxes and sell the rest of our land, and that our family would have to hire ourselves out to other families. If this happened our name might disappear from the families of Israel.

Part 2 – Narrative of a pre-teen today – Brad Johnson

Now let's consider the kinds of answers we might hear from kids today. Meet Brad Johnson.

Brad's bio: Brad lives in a middle-class Christian home in the suburbs of Atlanta. He is 12 years old and has an eight-year-old sister. His dad works as a regional sales rep for P&G and his mom works part-time teaching preschool. He goes to Roswell Middle School and his grandparents on his dad's side live in Richmond, Virginia. His other grandma recently moved into an apartment near their home where his mom can help care for her.

Please describe your family. My parents are nice but a little strict, and my sister is totally annoying. My mom helps me with my homework and my dad helps coach my little league team in the spring.

Who are your heroes? Huh, I haven't thought about that before. I guess a few of the baseball players on the Braves are pretty cool.

What do you want to do when you get older? I'm not sure. I'll probably go to college and have to decide then, but I think I want to be a pro baseball player.

What is your family hoping to accomplish this year? Uh, I think we want to go on another vacation to Florida this summer and maybe get a new car.

What would you like to accomplish this year? I hope to be a pitcher on my baseball team this spring, and to make more friends at school. I really hope I get the new iPhone for Christmas.

What is your biggest hope? That the Braves make it to the World Series and that this cute girl at school will notice me.

What is your biggest fear? That I won't have any friends at school and will be treated like a nerd by the popular kids.

Now obviously these are fictional accounts I invented, but these pictures are not far from the mark. The first thing to notice is from where the kids get their identity. In the classical family, the sense of family identity was very strong—strong enough to be the primary force shaping the child's view of him or herself. Today, family identities are typically short-lived, not extending back generations, but kids still need to find their identity somewhere.

So what replaces the family as kids' identity-shaping agent? Usually it's their peers. If their peers think they're cool, then our kids think they're cool—and if their peers think they're a nerd, our kids believe think they're a nerd. The family is often powerless in combating these peer-based identity labels because the family identity is so weak.

As I've studied these two views of family, the striking difference that stands out is that in a classical family every person understands who they are in the context of the family. Each family member is seen as part of a cohesive team. I like to describe this redeemed, biblical model of the classical family as "Family Teams."

God has designed each Family Team to work together, and each person in the family—father, mother, son, daughter, grandpa, grandma, brother, sister, uncle, aunt and cousin—has a very important and clear role to play that provides the grounding of their family identity.

So let's dive into the most basic questions about family, and try to understand what a modern western family believes, contrasted with the beliefs that come from being a Family Team.

HOW IMPORTANT IS THE FAMILY?

"My heart is filled with bitter sorrow and unending grief for my people, my Jewish brothers and sisters. I would be willing to be forever cursed—cut off from Christ!—if that would save them."
Romans 9:2-3

One way to discover whether or not you're prioritizing family over your individual desires is to examine how you feel when the family "takes" more from you than it gives in return. What happens when you have to make real sacrifices for the family? What if you feel the family is holding you back?

For most westerners, these circumstances often lead to resentment and frequently result in the abandonment of the family. Ongoing, genuine, individual sacrifices made for the family might even feel unhealthy to us. "It's *your* life," we are told. "You only go around once." And when we do choose to make sacrifices for family members, these sacrifices are often more motivated by the strength of our relationships with them as an individual than by viewing sacrifice as a natural part of what it means to be a member of a family.

In a Family Team, you see yourself primarily as a part of a family, and not just as an individual. And just like any other team, when the team scores, you all score, even if you weren't a direct part of that particular play. Conversely, if the team loses, you all lose, even if you played your best game.

Team identity is extremely powerful. Being part of a team is often the only time westerners experience an identity that, for a moment, trumps their own individual identity. And if you've ever been on a team that won a championship— through great individual sacrifices—you probably treasure that as one of the highlights of your life. What would happen if we all viewed family in the same way?

In the famous Christmas movie *It's a Wonderful Life,* George Bailey sacrifices his career for his younger brother and the rest of his dreams for the family business. But when things go south for him personally, he wants to die. He is then shown how different his family and his town would be without his individual sacrifice, which demonstrates to him how much he is loved and appreciated. It's one of the great tearjerkers of all time because, even though we live in a world that's often confused about self-sacrifice for the family, somehow we recognize that it's a beautiful thing.

Consider that this classic movie took place at a point in time when most people, for the first time in history, were beginning to believe in the superior value of the individual over the family. This shift was occurring in a cultural context where millions of people were making enormous, life-long individual sacrifices for their family, and this was seen as a virtuous. So which path did our culture take?

Something dramatically changed starting in the 1960s. People in all generations have been selfish, but during that period we began to believe collectively that putting yourself above the group was a virtue. On January 20, 1961 when JFK implored, "Ask not what your country can do for you, ask what you can do for your country," he seemed to see where things were heading. And the family has been the biggest casualty of this value shift. But each generation gets to consider anew which values they want to keep from the previous generation and which they want to restore.

You and your family need to consider this question deeply: will our family restore the ideal of making individual sacrifices to build a great family? This restoration begins with having a crystal-clear picture for the purpose of the family.

Digging Deeper

- [Movie] The Incredibles by Pixar: How a western family rediscovers how to work as a team
- [Movie] It's a Wonderful Life: How George Bailey plays the roles of son, husband, brother and father to their fullest and discovers that it's enough for a deeply meaningful life.

If you are reading the physical copy of this book you can find the links to the digging deeper resources at familyteams.com/FR.

WHAT IS THE PURPOSE OF THE FAMILY?

"God blessed them and said to them, "Be fruitful and multiply; fill the earth and subdue it. Rule..." **Genesis 1:26**

Whether in literature or movies, there's nothing quite like a good origin story. Understanding the beginning of a story illuminates and explains all the small details that can otherwise seem insignificant or puzzling. We experience this dynamic in personal relationships, as well. Once we learn someone's backstory, our relationship with them goes to the next level since we can begin to predict what might uniquely bring them pain or joy.

The same principle applies to family. We think we know what a family is, but most of us have lost our connection with its origin story. So cultures iterate and innovate on the concept of family without being tethered to its original purpose.

Before long, we find we've collectively drifted so far from the foundational ideas that undergird the idea of family that we can't find our way back. Fortunately for believers in the Bible, we have an account of the purpose statement given to the family the moment it came into existence.

Let's go all the way back to Genesis 1. God creates the family—the first man and woman—in verses 26 and 27, and then gives this first family its original mission statement in verse 28 when he says, "Be fruitful and multiply; fill the earth and subdue it. Rule over the fish in the sea and the birds in the sky and over every living creature that moves on the ground."

The first thing to notice is who makes the statement. If the purpose was dreamed up by the humans themselves, then an argument could be made that family was left undefined by God and perhaps it's up to us to come up with its purpose. But this is not what happened. God spoke the purpose over the first family, and as the Creator of the family, he had the prerogative to define its purpose. And similar to marriage where we read, "What God has brought together, let no man separate," whatever God establishes, humans lack the authority to change.

When I consider the mission given to the family and then look at the purpose imagined by modern western families, it's easy to see where we've diverged from the blueprint. We tend to think of a family's purpose as providing a nurturing environment. Our most common analogy for the family is the nest. Family is important as long as the chicks need protection during their long period of development, and the family begins to lose relevance once independence is achieved.

In contrast to this analogy, the original mission indicates that the family is designed not only to *be* an environment, but also to *do* something. Consider the verbs embedded in the mission statement: multiply, be fruitful, fill, subdue and rule. Our culture has a great word for a group that comes together for the purpose of accomplishing something—we call that thing a *team.* Families are designed to function like a team as they grow in number (multiply), deepen in quality (are fruitful), expand (fill), create order (subdue) and lead (rule). That's what God designed the family to do.

So how did we get sidetracked by the idea of the nest? Well, it's safe to assume we all want to be a part of a family characterized by nurturing and affection. There's nothing quite like entering a home full of joy, peace and intimacy, where the soft glow of candles illuminates a table full of good food and the faces of happy family members. Being a nest is a good thing, but this is not the goal of the family—it's a byproduct of another pursuit.

Our culture is trying to recover from this same error with regard to the purpose of the individual. For decades we've heard people say the purpose of life is to be happy. The pursuit of happiness is so American that it's in the Declaration of Independence. It seemed obvious as the purpose of life, simply because it's something we all wanted.

But the more we pursued happiness as our purpose, the more elusive achieving real happiness became. Depression increased, individuals became more and more narcissistic, willing to sacrifice anyone and anything in their pursuit of happiness.

If the feeling of happiness is your ultimate goal, you'll never achieve it. That's because happiness is a byproduct of pursuing meaningful goals—of serving something bigger and more important than yourself. Happiness was not designed to be pursued as an end in itself.

The same principle applies to family. Our goals must be founded on serving something beyond ourselves and our own narrow self-interests. God knew this back in Genesis 1 and gave family a meaningful purpose to pursue that was bigger than either the individual or the family.

If you want a family full of love and happiness—one that stays together and looks out for one another—you need to pursue meaningful goals as a team. In the midst of this pursuit is where you learn the self-sacrifice that's necessary as the foundation of a loving, nurturing environment.

But how do we shift our thinking to begin considering family as a team? It might help to consider that every team has diverse positions. These positions or roles must be well understood before the team takes the field. So let's take a deeper look at the parts that make up the Family Team.

THE COLLISION OF IDENTITIES

After reading the stories of Yitzach and Brad, it's helpful to consider how the mother, father and children in these two different families think about their roles in the family.

The Identity of the Father

"Children born to a young man are like arrows in a warrior's hands.
How joyful is the man whose quiver is full of them!" **Psalm 127:4-5**

Throughout history, men have been driven by the need to feel significant. They tend to ground their identities and put their greatest energies toward those things that provide them with that significance. In western culture, in particular, we know that men tend to get their strongest identity from their work. Why is this? Why do we want to know about a man's job immediately upon meeting him, and only much later ask about his family, if at all?

This work-based identity as distinct from one's family identity is a modern phenomenon that didn't exist in the same way in the past, and is still resisted in many cultures around the world today. This western shift is a result of the weakening of our family identities and the strengthening of the identity of the individual. Today a man could have an amazing career, leave his family in ruins and still be considered a truly great man. As a culture we have decided that individual achievement is vastly more important. While family can be seen as merely part of one's individual accomplishment, it's at most just a sub-point of a man's life and doesn't define him in any special way.

Remember 12-year-old Brad Johnson from our earlier illustration? If you were to ask Brad's dad where he gets his identity, what do you think he would say?

In our story, Brad has what we would tend to think of as a good, attentive dad. He provides for his family, spends time with his kids, and makes some real sacrifices for their benefit.

But like almost all western dads, Brad and his father seem to relate to each other primarily as two individuals. Why is this?

Why do Western dads struggle so much-with-deeply identifying with the family, abandoning and neglecting their families in numbers never before seen while dads in other cultures feel such a bond with their families? I don't believe it's as simple as dads in other cultures love their individual children more than dads on the West. In fact, men like Brad's dad are often very sensitive to their kids in ways beyond what you typically see in non-western cultures. But a huge difference is non-western dads often see their work identity as integrated with their family identity (they go to work to expand their multigenerational family) and western dads see their work identity as wholly distinct from their role as a father.

So western fathers face a different kind of dilemma when the needs of their children collide in a major way with their other desires—especially opportunities that are more likely to make him feel significant, like career advancement or a new romantic interest. He might try his best to find a way to fulfill both, but when a true conflict arises, he will either let his family take the hit or he will choose to take the hit himself— and consequently feel like a part of him has died.

But Yitzach's father experiences family in a totally different way. He views all of his life as a subset of family life. His identity is totally and completely intertwined with—and is inseparable from—his family. He's the father. He's the patriarch. He doesn't have a deeper or more significant identity.

If you consider Brad and Yitzach's families and ask who in each family is most likely to think more often about the family as a whole, you might find yourself coming to a surprising conclusion. I've asked this question many times and the answer I receive most often is that in Brad's family the person who thinks about the family constantly is the mother, but in Yitzach's family it is just as likely to be his father. Why is that?

Yitzach's dad sees his individual identity primarily as a subset of his family identity. His family is an inseparable part of him and he is a part of his family.

This doesn't solve every family problem, and even gives rise to new challenges, but imagine for a moment how much more of a secure environment this creates for children. Recent stats have reported that 60% of children in the United States will spend some or all of their childhood living apart from their biological father.

This level of father-neglect is impossible to imagine in a culture holding a classical philosophy of family, but it's unsurprising in a western context. The adoption of a western philosophy of family has done more to destroy the lives of children than any other single cause. A father in the classical paradigm identifies at a far deeper level with his children as his children. Thinking of abandoning his family would be like imagining cutting off his right arm because he sees each of them as part of himself.

In addition to his identity being so intricately tied up with his fathering, he would see building family as a central element of his purpose in life. A father who sees himself as a member of a family team views work as a part of how he is helping his family succeed, not as a separate endeavor around which he builds his own individual identity. Every morning when he goes to work, it's as if his family is sending him out on a mission to strengthen them by bringing back resources. And since a Family Team thinks about family multigenerationally, this father prizes efforts that will provide for his family—not only in his lifetime, but also long after he's gone. He wants to secure assets, and therefore opportunity and stability, that can be passed down to his children and his children's children. Family is his primary team.

Today modern corporations have done much to provide a sense of team spirit, where a man feels he is leading or is part of a corporate team, with the primary identity of employee of the corporation. But a classical father could never view work in this way. He is already on a team and he is working for his family, no matter what type of job he has. To make his family pay the price so he can serve a corporation at his family's expense would be to switch family teams.

These two fathers could not be more different. Both are good men, but they view family as radically different things:

One is providing for and enjoying his family as one of many detached elements that make up his individual life. The other is building his family as the primary identity through which he builds a meaningful life.

One sees family as a thing in which he is choosing to participate. The other sees family as an inseparable part of who he is.

One sees his family as something that started when he made a personal choice to get married and have children. The other sees family as something into which he was born—something that has been going on for thousands of years and that has been entrusted to his care for a time. He understands that his family is a bigger reflection of his life, not merely a small expression of it.

Once believers in Jesus begin to understand the power of this identity, they rightly start to wonder if this will lead to family becoming an idol. Isn't this just trading the idol of individualism for the idol of family?

This is a serious danger which we will discuss in further detail, but remember, at this point in our discussion we're building the foundation for what a classical family is—not the way the Gospel redeems the classical family. Jesus challenged the classical family in many ways but his solution was not to destroy the family or replace the classical family with the modern family. He insisted that those who receive the Gospel submit to his Lordship over everything else including the family.

The Identity of the Mother

"Strength and dignity are her clothing, And she smiles at the future." **(Proverbs 31:25)**

What compels many mothers to love and nurture their children is so powerful and instinctual that moms throughout the world tend to care for their families despite the prevailing philosophies of their cultures. This is an enormous blessing, because babies could be neglected and dying at a horrendous rate if something as simple as a philosophical shift could cause moms to stop loving and caring for their children.

But moms also need to understand the ways these cultural ideas impact the hearts of their husbands and their children. A mom I recently met expressed to me that dads just need to be trained to nurture and love their kids more, believing this will solve everything. But while this approach will often work very well with moms, it frequently fails with dads whose temperaments and drives are designed differently.

So in contrasting Brad's mother and Yitzach's mother, one big difference will be that Brad's mom will often feel she is leading and loving the family by herself. Western moms who sacrifice their bodies to have children and then their lives to raise them often struggle with feeling isolated and under-resourced. If the father doesn't value his family above himself, and if their kids are being raised to think of their individual needs above the family, a mother, seeking to put the family above her personal needs, can find herself fighting alone to save a ship long after everyone else has abandoned it.

In *The Godfather II,* Michael Corleone is trying to run his father's vast Mafia empire, but with a western marriage. He goes to his mother, who grew up in the old world, and asks, "Could Papa, by being strong for his family—could he—lose it?"

His mother seems so surprised that she doesn't even really understand the question. She simply responds, "But you can never lose your family."

Michael looks away and says to himself, "Times are changing."

In Michael's mother's classical family, everyone identified so deeply with the family that stresses tended to drive the family closer together. But in a western family, where everyone has opted into the family to get something out of it, stresses tend to blow the family apart.

It's important to understand this is not because classical people are better or more loving than western people. It's simply because they identify so deeply with their family that these stresses and attacks are not seen merely as a personal threat but as a collective one, causing the family to unite to defend itself. You are your family—that is how Michael's mother thinks. So you can't lose your family without losing your very self.

This means that when a husband begins to identify more and more with his family, a mother will begin to experience her role as a part of a team, instead of the family being her own private project. As her husband shows leadership and begins to set a vision—and to work with and through his family instead of apart from it—she will be deeply impacted by this team spirit and discover, often for the first time, the true and deepest purpose of her feminine nature. Instead of being the only one who sacrifices, she will see her husband laying down his life to love her and their children. When the husband and wife enjoy God's design for the family, they experience increasing oneness.

The Identity of the Children

"...the glory of children is their fathers." **Proverbs 17:6**

How do the children in our example, Yitzach and Brad, think of themselves? From where do they get their identities?

It's clear that almost all of Yitzach's identity comes from his family. He sees himself as a son of his father first and foremost. Even the way his name is constructed—Yitzach son of Asa—demonstrates that the root of his identity is in his multigenerational family through the father.

As a result, Yitzach doesn't need to "find himself." He knows who he is, even at a pretty young age. This is one of the reasons he can become a man at thirteen years old. The process of adolescence, during which young people struggle to discover and express their identity, culminates for Yitzach during a three-hour event called a Bar Mitzvah where he is given his identity as a man of the family.

The DNA of Yitzach's identity flows from his sonship. And this doesn't mean he is unable to put his unique stamp on his family. On the contrary, the family needs his unique skills and talents, as one day he will take a leadership position and be responsible for giving further definition and direction to the family vision. Every wedding, every Sabbath, every festival—every time he works or learns—is an occasion to deepen both his own family identity and his understanding of the family vision.

So what about Brad Johnson? How does he figure out who he is? When he goes to school or off to his first job, can Brad lean on his family identity because of his father's reputation? Not in western culture. Being a Johnson says next to nothing to his peers about who he is, and therefore it says nothing to Brad about who he is.

So who is Brad then? The plain truth is: Brad doesn't know who he is. According to his culture, his parents actually feel they are doing him a favor by giving him time and space to figure out his identity for himself.

How does a person find who they are, anyway? Current culture seem to assume we can teach kids to be whomever they want to be. But identity has to flow from something outside of us. It mostly needs to be given to us. I can tell the world, "I'm an artist," but what if the world fires back and says, "No, you're not." Who do I believe?

"Just believe in yourself," we're told. But this rarely works. And in the few cases when it does, this gives rise a much worse problem. We have a name for someone who can convince themselves of anything and remain defiantly unresponsive to societal or community feedback: a sociopath.

A sociopath is someone unaffected by the thoughts and feelings of others, who uses their emotional independence to manipulate others in order to get what they want.

But Brad isn't a sociopath and he knows he needs help from others to help him understand who he is, especially while he is young. So he pays very close attention anytime others label him, because he is desperately trying to discover who he is.

That is why he is so afraid of being called a nerd by the popular kids at school. That is why, as soon as his peers put him into a group and give him a name, that name may echo in his mind for the rest of his life. Because, right now, Brad is just Brad—and that doesn't tell him anything about who he really is. Is he Brad the nerd, Brad the athlete, Brad the artist, Brad the dork?

He's been given the great gift of western society—the blank slate, the ability to invent himself—but in reality that blank slate isn't in his hands. It's largely in the hands of his peers, who are free to write whatever they want to write on it about who they think he is. And whatever is written there during Brad's young life will likely be the identity he adopts throughout his adolescence. And since these messages are so powerful, Brad's adolescence might extend for many years, even into his thirties. Once he tires of the struggle to "find himself," he will most likely just give up, settle down, and try to come to peace with the confusion.

Is this God's design? Is having a weak family identity and a strong individual identity really helping our children? Let me mention here that there are clearly strengths to be gained by rooting individual identity in what the individual excels at. This is why western society produces many amazingly gifted individuals. But why can't we help children discover those individual strengths while being rooted in an identity of a strong family, instead of casting them out into the world where we know other rootless children will use our child's lack of identity as a way of strengthening their own?

One example of a classical family pattern that needs to be reconsidered is the inequality between sons and daughters and the role of the first-born over the other children. In the past there may have been survival reasons for these preferences. If the father split his inheritance with all of the children, and didn't give most of it to his firstborn son, the family might grow weaker with the more children they would have, and with every generation. This created a huge security risk for the whole family—especially the most vulnerable members of the family.

This was overcome by giving a much larger share to the firstborn son, so that he could keep the family safe and together, but this also had the effect of creating deep feelings of unfairness and rivalry for younger sons and for any daughters. This is one example of a classical family pattern we need to rethink in today's society where the physical security of the family is less of a concern.

We have a choice, even in western culture, to give our children a strong identity rooted in their family. We'll explore in detail the kinds of things that provide children with that strong family identity, but we must start by believing this is of extreme importance, because it won't be easy. But the quality of our children's lives will greatly depend on it.

Digging Deeper

- [Book] Hold On to Your Kids: Why Parents Need to Matter More Than Peers: An exploration from two secular psychologists of the impact of Western parents obsession with fostering peer-orientation

in their kids.
- [Article] <u>The Power of Family History Study</u> by Emory University

If you are reading the physical copy of this book you can find the links to the digging deeper resources at <u>familyteams.com/FR</u>.

The Identity of Siblings

"…a brother is born to help in time of need." **Proverbs 17:17**

As you begin to create a stronger family team, you'll notice one of the facets of identity that transforms the fastest is how siblings view one another.

A western family is a source from which members draw resources to meet their individual needs. So if a son, for example, has attentive and loving parents, he knows he can get most of his needs met through those relationships. But how will he view his sister? She can offer him very little; in fact, since she's drawing the same resources from the family that he wants (the attention of the parents, money, a private bedroom, etc.), he might perceive her to be a liability, and every subsequent child born into the family makes resources even more scarce. This is one reason many western families have fewer children—the more children the less each receives.

As a result of this scarcity mindset, many siblings view each other as rivals, with little reason to be patient with each other's flaws and quirks. Though parents will often strive to give equal individual attention and resources to each child, the scarcity mentality remains; often children will wait until they leave the house (and the threat is minimized) before they'll consider pursuing friendships with one another.

But if the family is viewed as a team, sibling identity is seen in a completely different light. A strong family team identity causes kids to view more children as assets instead of liabilities—the team gets stronger with each child born. Each new child's strengths and resources are added to the collective family resources. This is especially true if the parents can foster the understanding that the family is a team for life.

The more clearly you can paint the picture of siblings as lifelong teammates, the easier it will be for the kids to overcome the times when they annoy one another. It's really important to find ways for siblings to work together on the same team as early as possible. They need to root for one another as a part of the family and not only as individuals. They need to celebrate together when the family scores. This simple shift will bring an incredible amount of peace, life and love into your home and will pay dividends for many generations.

Digging Deeper

- [Movie] Thirteen Days. John and Bobby Kennedy work as a team to solve the Cuban missile crisis.
- [Movie] Children of Heaven. Iranian film where a poor brother and sister sacrifice for one another so they both can have a pair of shoes.

If you are reading the physical copy of this book you can find the links to the digging deeper resources at familyteams.com/FR.

The Identity of the Extended Family

"Grandchildren are the crowning glory of the aged..." **Proverbs 17:6**

Trying to decide how to incorporate extended family is often deeply confusing for western families. How often do I need to visit Grandma? Am I responsible for my cousin who's having a hard time? Should I go to the annual family reunion? Many of us end up deciding based on whether or not these relationships would still be important to us if they were not family. If the answer is yes, then we treat them like we would any other friend, and if the answer is no, then the relationship begins to drop down the priority scale. Why not? You don't owe them anything. You might experience occasional feelings of guilt or regret, but it's hard to understand why or what to do about it.

On the other hand, the more deeply a person believes in the classical family perspective, the more they will make major sacrifices for extended family members. Why the difference?

First, this seems to stem from a deep sense of shared identity within the same family line. Members of classical families understand the special significance that comes from sharing a common family story. But this requires that extended family members *know* and identify with the larger family story.

In my family, in order to make sure our own family story is known, we host a special dinner every month with my wife's family—and another dinner for my side of the family—that gives our parents the opportunity to share family stories with their grandkids, usually complete with pictures, lessons and some entertaining Q&A. The more cousins, aunts and uncles from each side that come and participate, the richer the experience for all of us.

By doing this, we are laying the groundwork for an extended family identity. Engendering a sense of belonging to a stronger, bigger, more diverse team is the second reason classical families tend to value extended family members. As our children begin to steward the family resources and further develop the family legacy, they will often need a larger number of teammates with which to participate. The more we succeed at fulfilling the family vision, the more they will need loving, loyal family members with an intuitive understanding of the family identity—and the various skills needed to help with all the diverse roles.

Finding a place in a larger extended family greatly helps children see they are part of something much bigger than themselves. And even when a child struggles with relating to their parents or siblings because their gifts or personality are especially unique, they can often find a member of the extended family who understands them, who can encourage them to serve the family, and who can model for them how their uniqueness is a special asset to the team.

Digging Deeper

- [Movie] My Big Fat Greek Wedding - A huge extended family with all its quirks working together

If you are reading the physical copy of this book you can find the links to the digging deeper resources at familyteams.com/FR.

THE FAMILY PLANNING FLIP

"Marry and have children. Then find spouses for them so that you may have many grandchildren. Multiply! Do not dwindle away!" - Jeremiah 29:6

Perhaps there's no area that demonstrates the contrast between western and classical family more starkly than the area of family planning. If I'm curious what someone's philosophy of family is, and I don't mind being invasive, all I need to do is ask the question, "So how do you guys decide when to have kids and how many to have?" Often within the first few seconds of answering this question, they clearly describe their entire family philosophy. This is because western and classical families have opposite approaches to the topic of family planning.

When most western couples gets married, it's assumed they are going to plan when to get pregnant. In premarital counseling we don't ask whether they've decided to plan their pregnancies, because we believe that not to plan feels terribly irresponsible to western people. Which is ironic, considering how recent widespread family planning really is. The responsible process, we believe, begins by enjoying married life for years without the imposition of children, then ensuring we have ample financial resources for another family member before we consider whether we'd like to have a child.

Classical people also think it's important to prepare the right environment for having children, but to them, that environment is simply marriage. Children don't need a freshly painted nursery; they just need a mother and father who have committed to a lifelong covenant of faithfulness. And while western families are keenly aware of the costs of having children too early, like missed career or travel opportunities, classical families are keenly aware of the costs of delay. Every year you wait to have children will be another year that child will not know their grandparents. Every year you hold off is a year you deepens in your individual identity instead of your family identity. And every year a couple delays reduces the number of children the family is able to have.

How do western families decide how many children to have?

One way of deciding was best summed up by evangelical minister Voddie Baucham: "A boy for me and a girl for you / then praise the Lord, we're finally through!" And if the first two kids are the same gender, then society grants you a pass to try one more time. But having a fourth child or more is when western people will begin to wonder if something is wrong with these parents who are often greeted with the tongue in cheek question, "Haven't you figured out what causes that yet?"

What's really driving these western decisions is the underlying question, "What is the smallest number of children we can have that will fulfill each of our individual desires?" If both careers are paramount values, then choosing to have no children is common (but with a dog thrown in at some point to enjoy nurturing something while maintaining a more convenient lifestyle). If the couple wants to experience parenthood, but in the absolutely most convenient way possible, than having one child will do. It's only when they want to experience having a child of both genders that having two or three kids makes sense.

In a classical family context, however, the basic belief was: more kids = more blessings. Each new child was considered a gift from God to the family. Children represented every family's social security and would be expected to care for their parents in their old age. Families worked together, often for life, so each child contributed financially to the family and were considered a financial asset instead of a liability. The fact that most western families no longer rely on their children to care for them or no longer work as a team are cultural decisions that have also totally transformed our attitudes toward children.

So much has changed since those times that it's surely worth exploring whether family planning should be reevaluated before adopting attitudes toward reproduction that are wholly classical. However, most of us are starting with deeply-held western beliefs about reproduction that have their origin in individualism instead of a biblical view of family and children. Be prepared to encounter thoughts and ideas in God's design for the family that challenge these sacred western assumptions as we dive deeper into how the Bible challenges our thoughts about the family.

WE NEED A NEW LENS

"But now, what about me? When can I start providing for my own family?" - **Genesis 30:30**

And now if you're completely confused about family planning, seeing the flaws in western individualism and classical collectivism, you'll understand why it's important to utilize a new lens through which we can understand God's design for the family. Attempting to bring back the classical family simply exchanges western family problems with classical family problems. So it's critical to understand that there is no way we can just reform or upgrade the western philosophy of family either, because its foundational beliefs that the individual trumps the family and the way they ignore the multigenerational family line oppose God's original design.

On the other hand, while the classical view of family has a clearer understanding of family identity and its high level of importance, it often turns into an idol that completely subjugates both God and the individual. How can we construct a truly biblical view of family considering how far we've drifted, especially in recent years?

Now that we have a better picture of the classical philosophy of family, we can begin to understand the world into which the Bible speaks. From the very first pages of Scripture, starting with the Torah (the first five books of the Bible) and throughout the rest of the Old Testament, the Bible teaches us how to bring the family under God's rule. From there, the New Testament uses the story of the Gospel to fully redeem the essence of family by illustrating the true spiritual picture that each family relationship reflects (marriage, adoption, sonship, fatherhood etc). So going forward our challenge is to rediscover a model of family that combines a basic understanding of the classical model and the fine-tuning of the family given in the Torah with the redemption and restoration of the family presented in the New Testament. This perspective on family could be called a multigenerational team on mission. We honor the multigenerational character of the family, we function like a team and we're on a mission of restoration given to us through the Gospel.

But is it reasonable to think we can express this idea of family in today's society? All our tools for building family life come from western culture and assume a western philosophy of family. We need to bring online a set of ancient tools, and we need to see how today's family might wield these tools to build a multigenerational team on mission. So let's explore just seven tools that are important to rediscover in order to build our family teams.

HOW TO BUILD A FAMILY TEAM

INTRODUCTION: COACH, MEET YOUR TEAM

"The total number of family leaders over the fighting men was 2,600…men trained for war, a powerful force to support the king against his enemies." **2 Chronicles 26:12-13**

We often hear that men just don't like being around children and I almost believed it until the fall of 2007 when I enrolled my then-seven-year old son Jackson in football. We pulled up to his first practice and I was shocked to see there were almost as many grown men as boys. Before Jackson even arrived at the part of the field where his team was practicing, he was greeted by several men and he spent the next three hours being coached by two dads who carefully trained him every detail of the basics. This seemed kind of crazy to me. My son was only seven! Watching this, it dawned on me that most men don't have a kid problem but a role confusion problem.

So here's a thought experiment to consider: imagine if a law was passed that every weekend each family would play a competitive game with other family teams. The only coaches are the family dads and the results would be posted publicly. What do you think would happen to many men's level of engagement with their families?

Just imagine if every father in the western world woke up one morning and completely forgot about their view of family. When they saw their wife and children all they saw was a team with three practices per week and a game every weekend. These fathers also believed their primary identity within their family was as the coach of this team, and both their standing in the community and their legacy as men depended on how well they developed and led their team to victory. This picture is about as close as a western man can get to understanding how the patriarchs Abraham, Isaac and Jacob viewed family. The coach/team analogy is not a perfect picture of the biblical family, but it can really help bridge the gap for modern men between the ancient world of the Bible and the modern western world.

Let's consider some of the elements ancient families and modern teams have in common.

- The success of the team depends on the skill and dedication of the coach.
- The coach needs to work with and develop the talent he's been given.
- Players come very raw, undisciplined and in need of serious training.
- When the players get sloppy or the coach gets lazy, the whole team suffers and loses heart.
- Good players think of themselves as part of team first and individuals second.
- If the coach abandons his team, the team immediately begins to unravel and fall apart.
- The coach learned coaching back when he was coached as a player on a team.
- Great coaches listen to and show affection for their players.
- A good coach discovers and releases players in their area of greatest strength and builds them up where they are weak.
- The coach must provide morale by demonstrating his commitment; the staff and players feed off his drive.

I'm not even a big sports fan, but I can tell you how much easier it is for me as a man to understand and get excited about this role compared to the abstract and ambiguous concept of the western dad. Coaches in our culture are highly respected and even revered. On the other hand, dads today are so often mocked, disrespected and demeaned by our culture. Coaches are expected to be strong and vision-driven. Dads are expect to be weak and confused. Coaches are expected to have a plan of action. Dads are expected to stay out of the way. Coaches are expected to spend many hours every week training their players. Dads are expected to be distracted by their work and hobbies and, at best, try to find some time to spend with the family when it's convenient. Isn't it crazy that we expect so much more out of a coach than out of a dad? But families are teams and dads are their coaches. Next time you meet a dad, instead of saying something like, "How're the wife and kids?" try saying, "How's your team doing?" Because if western dads ever began to really understand who they are, millions of them would rise up and be outstanding leaders in their families. So many of them, even those who have come from tough families themselves, have it in them to be amazing coaches. They're just terribly confused about who they are and what their family is.

So let's start to change that. Below are seven tools the Bible gives us that will help moms and dads begin to transform their disconnected family into a team. You don't need to do all seven but the more of these you begin to implement, the stronger your family identity will become. Almost all these tools have been abandoned in the west, so let's assume that we are starting from scratch—I'll do my best to make each one very practical so you can pick up these tools and go to work building your own family team.

TOOL #1 -
THE VALUE
OF FAMILY

What happens when individual and family interests collide? Western culture, by default, tends to side with the individual, which is one reason western families are so weak. Countless movies have been made in the past fifty years whose theme is the individual learning to put their own interests above their family's. Sure, there are times when that is necessary and right—families should also be prepared to make great sacrifices for the individual—but as a default setting, this is extremely dangerous. The story of the immigrant family sacrificing everything to see the first child from the family gets a college degree, only to watch the newly minted individual spend that investment on their own individual interests while the family stands back in confusion and disbelief has become a common East-meets-West story. How do we find a way to properly order these two competing values?

THE BIBLE'S VALUE FOR THE FAMILY

Grant Me a Son

"Abram replied, "O Sovereign Lord, what good are all your blessings when I don't even have a son?" **Genesis 15:2**

What is Abram's problem?

When God comes to him in Genesis 15 and tells him that He will protect him and give him a great reward, Abram snaps back that no reward matters if he fails to have children. Hearing a reply like Abram's immediately makes me wince, anticipating a harsh rebuke from God. But no rebuke comes. God rebukes Abram at other times in the book of Genesis, but here He gently replies, "...you will have a son of your own who will be your heir." Then the Lord takes Abram outside and says to him, "Look up into the sky and count the stars if you can. That's how many descendants you will have!"

What's going on here? For years I blew off this scene as just some primitive obsession for offspring that people had in ancient times that we overcame. We now know that the power to have kids is really no big deal. You get married, then you have kids (and hopefully not too many). I've even joked with my kids, "You better be good or I'll get rid of you and make another one that looks just like you." (Yep, I'll be paying counseling bills for that one). So how big of a deal is it that we have the ability build families and have kids?

As I mentioned in the "My Story" section above, the first time I began to question my assumption that this kind of value for family and children was more than an unfortunate relic of ancient history was when I saw it played out in modern families in Israel. In the Israeli movie Ushpuzin, a 21st-century religious Jewish couple is getting along in years and cries out for the Lord's blessing in many parts of their lives. As the movie progresses, this older couple occasionally and only very gently talks about their acceptance of the fact that they can't ever have children. You get the feeling that even discussing it would be too painful. But in the last scene (spoiler alert!) you're taken to a room of explosive celebration where all the characters in the movie dance around the couple's eight-day-old son. How many western movies have a climax like that? Our climaxes are mostly based on romantic love or individual achievement. The boy finally gets the girl, the general wins the war, the weaker hero overcomes the stronger villain. But when was the last time you saw a movie that climaxed when the barren woman gives birth to her first child? Why does this couple care so much about having a kid? The simplest reason, in a single word, is Abraham.

Jewish people who value the Torah (the first five books of the Old Testament), like the Jewish family in the movie, have a faith deeply shaped by the characters in the Torah, and Abraham is one of the Torah's primary characters. But while modern orthodox Jewish families tend to share the Torahic view of the high value for offspring Christians values around offspring seem to view children through a secular cultural lens.

Sometimes Christians (including myself) have tried to write off the divergence between Jewish and Christian viewpoints on children as an Old vs New Testament difference. There are two major problems with this approach. One is that the Old Testament was actually the primary teaching curriculum of the Christians in the first century. When Paul wrote in 2 Timothy 3:16 that "All Scripture is breathed out by God and profitable for teaching, for reproof, for correction, and for training in righteousness" the word "Scripture" was talking about the Old Testament. The second is the implicit assumption that the Holy Spirit changed His mind about the importance of family between the Old and New Testament. We'll see shortly that both Testaments actually teach the exact same thing about the value of family. No, if we want to hold onto our current understanding that children really aren't always a blessing as Abram thought they were, then we're believing that western ideas of family are superior to those believed by father Abraham.

So we can see that Abram thought children were extremely important, but now we need to turn to answering the question why.

Individual Rights vs. Family Responsibility

"My husband's brother refuses to carry on his brother's name in Israel." - Deuteronomy 25:7

Have you ever read a passage in the Bible and been embarrassed by something it says? Ever wondered if the Bible's editors really missed it when they forgot to delete or at least reword a particularly shocking passage.

Whenever you find a statement or concept you would have removed if God put you in charge of editing the Bible, immediately pause. This is the moment you will discover if you believe the Bible is the Word of God or a book that reinforces your own personal religion. Believers who really trust the Bible will spend much more time trying to understand and shape their lives to hard truths, while those who use the Bible for their own ends will quickly pass by hard passages since they don't fit their own ideas.

Let's deal with one of the passages that deeply embarrasses western Christians. Deuteronomy 25:5-10 describes what to do when a man dies without having any children. It says that if he has a brother living with him on the family land, then his widow must marry that brother in order to produce an heir so that his name is not blotted out from Israel.

But the most shocking thing about this passage is who gets the most angry if the living brother chooses not to produce an heir for his dead brother: the widow. It's the widow fighting for her rights that is the basis for this law. It's the widow who is wronged if the brother refuses to fulfill his duty. Far from being a passive pawn between two selfish men, if the living brother refuses, the widow takes his brother-in-law before the elders, spits in his face, takes off his sandal and gives the brother's family a disgraceful name they will carry with the family forever.

What is going on here? What you see, on many levels, is what happens when individual rights collide with family responsibility. Reading this part of the Torah, we wonder what God expects his people to do when faced with this very common collision? Does the individual get their way or does the individual need to sacrifice for the family?

As Christians, we know that we no longer live under the law and that we no longer can be in the same circumstances as this widow who must produce an heir or the family will lose their name and ancestral land. But let's look at what made the widow so angry. She wasn't fighting for herself and she wasn't even fighting for her dead husband—she was fighting for the survival of her multigenerational family. This is not a story about how men subjugate women; it is a story about how both men and women naturally and voluntarily subjugate themselves for their family. The passage gives us her motive when it tells us she is offended because her brother-in-law refuses to "carry on the name of the dead brother so that his name will not be blotted out from Israel." During tool number two we'll discuss family lineage in detail, but for now let's try to grasp the level of sacrifice God expected from His people when it came to protecting and serving their future families. This kind of sacrifice could only come when husbands/fathers and wives/mothers completely identify with their family line. Western people actually do understand this kind of sacrifice for country. We honor the soldier who voluntarily gives his life to gain freedom for generations of his fellow countrymen, but we can struggle if anyone gives their life voluntarily for the future generations of their family.

Families are not only an extension of our lives as individuals, but they are also an extension of the thousands who have come before us and the possible thousands who will come after us. Compared to their collective needs, our momentary wishes become much smaller. This widow is a hero to her future family. She models for us the extent to which we as both men and women need to be prepared to serve our families. And although I'm glad we no longer need to follow this particular practice to protect ancestral land rights, we all need to be prepared to give up many of our individual desires to serve our family in ways that challenge western culture.

But does this turn family into an idol? Does the New Testament present a different vision of individual over family? Let's take a look.

Family Responsibility vs. Responsibility to God

"Anyone who does not provide for their relatives, and especially for their own household, has denied the faith and is worse than an unbeliever." **1 Timothy 5:7**

Christians in western culture who are deeply committed to God and His Kingdom tend to struggle constantly with balancing their family responsibilities and their ministry calling. Western Christians tend to live their lives through a series of isolated compartments, one for work, one for family, one for God, and one for themselves, etc. Their lives then become a constant battle of ordering priorities, with God rightfully on top. But this is why so many of the most driven Christian ministers in Western culture tend to say, at the end of their lives, something like "I regret that I didn't spend more time with my family" (Christianity Today interview with Billy Graham). Something had to give, and the family is often what that takes the hit.

Why is this so common? Why do those who seem to pour their heart and soul into God's work, like pastors and missionaries, have a reputation for neglecting the raising of their kids? I'd like to discuss one reason not normally considered, which came to light the more I spent time with families in the Middle East. Our imbalanced beliefs and actions about the family stem directly from our collective tendency to ignore the Old Testament as a source for practical life lessons and to draw the answers to our questions about how to live exclusively from the New Testament. They are two parts of a complete whole and they need each other. And to show you exactly what I mean, let me ask you to count all the specific children of New Testament leaders mentioned in the Bible.

I'm a dad of five kids who does a lot of ministry every week, so where can I go in the New Testament to find a model for how to balance family and ministry? You don't need to be a New Testament scholar to realize that it takes less than one finger to complete this assignment. Where does a dad go when he wants to find a model of a good father? The New Testament narratives are full of profiles of single men on mission for God's Kingdom and the Old Testament is full of narratives of families living in God's Kingdom. Which Testament will give you more answers to all of your practical questions about balancing family and ministry? Most Christian families in full-time ministry are entirely unaware of the helpful instruction they can receive from these Old Testament families.

Do the Old and New Testaments contradict one another? No. Instead, they perfectly complement each other, because Old Testament stories almost exclusively deal with the family narrative while New Testament stories almost exclusively present a single, missionary narrative. But when the New Testament discusses family, it's clearly doing so from the context of the Old Testament. So when someone reads only the Gospels and Acts to try and figure out how to live a balanced life, they might be tempted to think, "I guess we're all supposed to quit our jobs, leave our families, and live like nomadic missionaries." If they are single, this would definitely be a biblical option, but if they have a family, they'll be surprised once they get to 1 Timothy 5. Here Paul is writing instructions for Timothy to give to the church at Ephesus, and the list of family commands reads like it came straight out of the Old Testament. He tells believers their "first responsibility" is to "repay" their parents and grandparents (1 Timothy 5:3) and that if they don't provide for their wife and kids, then they've denied the faith and are worse than an unbeliever.

What faith have they denied? The faith based only on stories of single guys on missionary journeys sleeping by the side of the road like we have in the Gospels and Acts? No, the faith of the Torah that outlines in detail the responsibilities of mothers and fathers. Let's consider what those responsibilities entail just from Paul's instruction. For someone like me who has both of his parents living, one grandmother, both of my wife's parents living, five kids, and a sister who is a single mom with two kids, I need to be prepared to shoulder the needs of 6 dependents in my immediate family and 8 more in my extended family. It's tough to provide for 14 people when you're a nomad on mission. So which comes first when these priorities collide? Who gets the resources? Will I be denying my faith if I go on mission and deny it in another way if I don't?

The good news is that both the Old and New Testaments have the same answer. Our first responsibility to God is our responsibility to our family. There is no tension, no compartments, no separate buckets, because these categories are an invention of our dis-integrated modern culture. Jesus himself taught this and lived it in His own life. Jesus interpreted the fifth commandment "to honor your father and mother," like most rabbis throughout history: you set aside money to provide for your parents in their old age. And when the Pharisees wanted to make an exception for people wanting to give the money as a special offering, Jesus told them this was wrong because it was against the clear command of the Torah (Mark 7:9-13). Jesus worked as a carpenter to provide for His family, possibly being the sole breadwinner for 15 years after his father's likely death (Matthew 13:54-55). And even while He hung in agony on the cross, Jesus fulfilled His duty to His mother by having His disciple John adopt her into his family (John 19:26-27).

Once again, the key to integration is through identity. I am not called to ministry apart from my family; I am my family and my family is me. We are inseparable. If God calls me to go on some unique mission and I'm married, then He's also calling my wife. And if we have kids, then He's calling them, too. The tales of single-minded pastors living like single men, working almost every night of the week to serve the church, should not inspire us—they should concern us. Because of their positions, these men are the models of how to live for the many believers under their care. The Scriptures label this kind of neglect a denial of the faith, both of our Torahic foundation and also disobedience from clear Apostolic instruction. These men are trying to take the gifts of married people (loyal, lifelong companionship, sex, children, etc.) and the gifts of single people at the same time (the difference is carefully outlined by Paul in 1 Corinthians 7). This is not a biblical option. We must find a way to bring all of our responsibilities as moms, dads, sons, daughters, sisters and brothers into alignment with the teaching of Scripture.

Tools for Raising our Value for Family

So now that we've looked at the biblical reasons why we value family, it's time to search for a few tools that will help make these ancient, lost ideas practical to a family living in the 21st century.

Build Team Spirit

"The Lord bless you, my daughter!" Boaz exclaimed. "You are showing even more family loyalty now than you did before..."
Ruth 3:10

If one of your children goes to watch a sporting event where their sibling is playing, how do they feel? Do they see this as one of the annoying drawbacks of having a brother or sister? Do they feel like, if there is any fairness in this world, their siblings better have to suffer through watching them for an identical amount of time? We western parents play right into this because we can get obsessively worried about fairness, believing the only way to keep peace in the home and to prevent siblings from hating each other is by continually re-balancing the scales. So during the game when the watching child complains about being bored, we pull out the family fairness ledger and tell them that their siblings will have to suffer through watching them at their sport or activity. We use this for everything from Christmas presents to bites of dessert. And while there is nothing wrong with working to ensure your kids don't feel left out, fairness is a dangerous basis for sibling relationships.

Why should we use caution when making these fairness arguments with kids or with ourselves?

Because we're teaching our kids that:

- The fewer siblings they have the more they get.
- Individual rights come before family needs.
- All of their siblings are solo players on opposing teams.
- Parents owe their kids equality in everything.

All these beliefs and attitudes come from our belief that the family exists primarily to meet the needs of individuals in an equitable way. But it's possible to turn all these beliefs and feelings on their heads, right here, in the middle of western culture, by redefining family as a lifelong team, as the most important, most exciting, most productive team your kids will ever join.

Imagine if your kids, watching that game, felt like every time their sibling scored, they scored, just like people feel when watching their favorite sports team. Imagine how it would feel for the child playing the game to have a whole section of the bleachers erupt louder than their teammates every time they made a good play. Do you see how this would teach our kids that:

- The more siblings we have, the more blessed we are.
- The family is more important than my individual achievements.
- All my siblings are on my team with me.
- Parents are my main coaches and are trying to do what's best for our team as a whole.

All of this is possible if you choose to build a family team, and building a team involves cultivating these attitudes.

First, you need to talk like you're a team. This begins with the coaches (read: parents). April and I often refer to our family as

Team Pryor. We reinforce this by using "we" language as often as possible. If one child scored, then "we scored." If someone achieves anything, whether it's a good grade or one of our businesses gets a new client, we always celebrate as a team, saying things like, "Yay for our team," and, "Look how God has blessed our family." Language is a huge key to making this belief stick. We must begin by purging all the individualistic language that has infected our vocabulary.

Second, you have to experience being a team. This takes some creativity and thought, because our culture wants to separate people into grades and ages, making it impossible for families to compete as a team. I did research for several months on different sports that would have the greatest chance of allowing our family to work like a team and I concluded that tennis could provide this experience. Kelsey and Jackson play as a doubles team against others and our next two, Sydney and Elisa, are being prepared to do the same. We take lessons as a family, and our kids are learning how to help each other, the older kids training the younger kids as everyone works together. It's been an amazing blessing. My wife and I didn't know the first thing about tennis, but this was one of the best decisions our family has ever made.

We still let our kids do team sports on occasion. I believe team sports are so helpful at giving kids the correct picture of teamwork, but tennis has a prime spot in our rhythm. It's our version of PE and allows us to build a family team while getting our exercise and having a great time. Other ideas for creating team experiences are going on an adventure like a hiking expedition, family missions trips or service projects.

Third, an essential part of every team, and one especially easy to neglect as a family team, is the debrief. After any big game, whether you win or lose, if the team wants to improve, it's critical for the coach to lead the team in a discussion of what worked and what didn't. This kind of debrief, if it happens frequently, can replace a lot of hectic and often counterproductive on-the-spot correction for older kids. I'm a fan of immediate correction for training young children, but older children are a totally different animal. By the time your child reaches six or seven, begrudging obedience should not be your goal. You must capture their heart. The debrief will both reveal the current state of your child's heart and it be a time to make heartfelt appeals to the importance of loving each other and behaving like a team.

At the end of a bad day, when there has been a lot of bickering, don't just go to bed and hope tomorrow gets better. Gather the family and discuss what happened and why. I'm always asking the kids questions like, "Would you guys rather have a family that fights and hurts one another until we all go crazy or a peaceful family where we love each other and look out for each other?" And if a kid ever rolls their eyes and tries to end the debrief through saying the right answer, don't let it slide. Step up and challenge that child. Help them see that each decision they make leads the family down one path or the other. It takes too much work to resist constant, loving encouragement from one's family. The hardness in our kids' hearts will routinely soften during these debriefs because they really do love each other and they really do love our family. This allows you to notice and address patterns and discuss alternate behavior at a time and place when the kids are more likely to be soft and ready to listen.

The last element I'll touch on briefly here (but much more in the section on roles) is that each member of the family must feel needed. If a team has lots of team spirit but a child never plays in the game, if they feel they have nothing to contribute and that they're a loser among winners, they will begin to lose heart. There are no benchwarmers in the family. God has placed each child in your family for a reason and that child's gifts must be discovered, enhanced, released and celebrated inside of the family team.

Quantity Time

"As Jesus was getting into the boat, the man who had been demon possessed begged to go with him. But Jesus said, "No, go home to your family..." **Mark 5:18-19**

There are two very different ways to view time with your family. One way is to see it as a compartment of your life to which you allocate time. If you spend time with your family in this way, you will never avoid the constant frustration that your family time is taking away from other important activities or that other important activities are taking away from family time. For working moms and dads, this involves long seasons where the family loses their best time and attention and those times can never be recaptured. We need to seriously consider another way.

What if you decide to live in, with and through your family? What if you reject family as one of the compartments of your life and see family instead as the environment in which you experience as much of your life as possible? The more I began to identify myself with my family, the more this felt like the natural way to live. But be aware, virtually all elements of western culture are set up to separate individuals from their families. Rejecting this requires building a very different kind of culture. However, when I consider God's design for the family and who he has called me to be as a father, I no longer believe treating family like a compartment is an option. Family is not a part of my life. My family is in me and I am in them and so we need to be deeply interconnected. To live like separate individuals is to deny this reality.

How is this possible in today's society? What does this look like? It begins by taking the elements of life that are compartments—work, worship, friendships, hobbies, learning etc.—and doing as many as possible with, in, through and as a family. Perhaps every day should be "take your child to work day." Maybe it means you don't separate and go into different groups to worship. You worship together, and even more importantly, you worship as a family in your home. Maybe it means your friends are friends of your family and that when you give your love and loyalty to a friend, you are giving that love and loyalty to their family. Maybe it means you either find ways to enjoy your hobbies with your family or you find new hobbies that your family can enjoy with you. Maybe it means that whenever someone in your family acquires a new skill, you complete the learning experience by sharing it with your family. But whenever possible you learn together.

We will explore each of these examples in detail in coming sections, but I want to point out here that this is completely different than making men, for example, feel guilty that they need to spend more time with their family. The design of western culture will make him fail. Maybe we need to consider a complete lifestyle redesign. We have to stop compromising with western culture and choose to begin the process of remaking it. Instead of asking the question, "how can I spend more time with my family." why not design each part of your life to be lived with your family, and if a part refuses to allow your family identity as husband and father, you can choose to begin to work to change it or get rid of it.

If an activity comes with the label "no wives or kids allowed," maybe that's more of a single man's activity. I'm always a father, not just on evenings and weekends. I'm a father and husband everywhere I go and in everything I do. Sure people are confused at first when I bring one or more of my kids to board meetings and pause to explain something to them, or when I take my whole family overseas with me on missions trips, or when I choose to play sports I can play with my kids, but I believe all these decisions were made when I chose to be a husband and father. I'm a part of a package and in every way this makes me a better person and it makes what I bring to the table in a relationship whether in business, ministry or my personal life far more extensive than if you only got detached little me. My wife and I are in the process of multiplying ourselves many times over.

Years ago when we started our first business, we went to apply for a line of credit at the bank. They gave April a personal financial statement worksheet and told her to list our assets on one side and our liabilities on the other, and since we didn't own anything at the time, we had nothing to write, so she looked up at the banker and said, "Well, we have kids." He pointed to the other side of the document and said, "Kids are a liability, not an asset." In that one phrase our banker stated, in the clearest way I've ever heard, why western families are designed to fail. We believe that kids are a liability. They make our life harder not better. They distract us from work, from worship, from fun, and our quality of life would be better if they never existed.

If you believe this is a lie, then prove it by investing your life into your children, beginning with integrating every part of your life possible into your common life as a family. Instead of thinking of work/life balance, we pursue the integrated life. This kind of lifestyle redesign may take years and it will likely change the way you do every area of your life, but I think you'll discover, as you take this path, that this is what you were made for.

Digging Deeper

- [Video] A Journey Home - The journey of the

Waller family when Tommy Waller left his demanding job with FedEx, bought land in Amish country, and began to live every part of his life with his family.

If you are reading the physical copy of this book you can find the links to the digging deeper resources at familyteams.com/FR.

TOOL #2 –
THE SCOPE OF FAMILY

Families are multigenerational.

One paradigm that has been almost entirely removed from western families is its identity as a multigenerational line. Losing this perspective has done untold damage to families, and over time this loss is being demonstrated through breakdowns in almost every part of our society. In America, for example, we have seen an egregious example of generational theft as the national debt continues to grow and is simply passed down from generation to generation. We also have an incarceration rate at a level never before seen in history as fatherless men, with no role models or training, turn to addictions and commit crimes. These systemic, societal problems have grown due in part to the decision to shrink the scope of the family from a multigenerational line to what we call the nuclear family.

THE BIBLICAL SCOPE OF THE FAMILY

The Bible is extremely clear that when God views you, He sees not just an individual but a family. And when He sees your family, He looks at it generationally. We don't get to pick how to define family. We didn't design the family and so we can't shrink its scope. Even if you don't like what you're about to learn about the scope of family, understand this is simply the only way the Bible describes it. For those who trust in the Bible as the source of truth, we must accept its definitions. But I also hope that you'll see the incredible wisdom of God in establishing this design and so find this not just acceptable to your head but also attractive to your heart as well.

God's Glory through Generational Connections

"I lavish unfailing love to a thousand generations...I lay the sins

of the parents upon their children...even children in the third and fourth generations." **Exodus 34:7**

Are all individuals really created equal? Of course, if we are asking if each person is born equally valuable, then the Bible answers a clear and undeniable, "Yes." Genesis 1 teaches that every person is created in God's image and that God's image is the basis for the value of all human life. But just as undeniable is the fact that not every person is born with equal opportunities. If you were born into a peasant family in rural Europe in the Middle Ages, do you have as equal a shot at a fulfilling life as someone born into a wealthy family in Toronto, Canada in the 21st century? Does someone born into a strict Muslim family in Saudi Arabia have exactly the same chance at believing the Gospel as someone born in a Christian family in the United States? These individuals are not experiencing equal opportunities. Why?

This can appear like a terrible design flaw in the way God made the world. Much of the modern western project is founded on the idea that, since every individual is equally valuable, society needs to be engineered in such a way to provide each individual with as close to equal opportunities as possible. So why didn't God engineer the world this way? Why not ensure that each individual has exactly the same opportunity at living a fulfilling, flourishing life? If you designed the world, would you give every individual equal opportunity from birth? It's hard to imagine a better or more fair way to make the world. What possible negative result could come from achieving the goal of the modern western project by providing equality in this way?

As far as I can tell there is only one valuable thing that would be destroyed if you achieved this goal and that is the multigenerational family. If families could do nothing to either help or hurt the next generation because they are all born with perfect equality no matter what the family did, then what would be the point in building a multigenerational family?

As terrible as it is to see a child born into a false religion or a country at war or to an abusive, addicted parent, the multigenerational family comes into existence because it has been given the gift of experiencing the cumulative result of the decisions of many generations. God designed the world to tell a multigenerational story instead of an individual story and western people have been trying to reengineer reality ever since. It feels unfair and it is unfair, if fairness is determined at the level of the individual. But it's not unfair at the family level. God has been clear about this from the beginning and He spelled out in detail his intention to design the world around multigenerational families 4000 years ago on a mountain in the Sinai desert.

Moses asks to see God's glory, a request both bold and dangerous. How can a sinful man see God's glory and live? But God decides to let Moses get as close to His glory as humanly possible. Hiding Moses in the cleft of a rock, God covers the entrance with His hand and passes by Moses declaring, in human language, the essence of His glory. Don't you wish you could know what God communicated to Moses in that moment? It could be the key to unlocking one of the greatest mysteries of the universe: what makes God so glorious. Well, actually, we know exactly what God said to Moses, and His description of His glory baffles the western mind so we rarely talk about it. He said this:

"Yahweh! The Lord!
　　The God of compassion and mercy!
　I am slow to anger
　　and filled with unfailing love and faithfulness.
　I lavish unfailing love to a thousand generations.

I forgive iniquity, rebellion, and sin.
But I do not excuse the guilty.
I lay the sins of the parents upon their children and grandchildren;
the entire family is affected—
even children in the third and fourth generations." (Exodus 34:6-7)

Yes, this is actually in the Bible. And not just conveniently buried in Leviticus (I do like Leviticus, by the way), but in a riveting narrative designed to highlight, italicize and underline who God is in His very essence. We need to deal with this not as something to explain away but something we must work to understand, believe and put our hope in.

God's ability to span the generations is one of His greatest attributes. Think about it. One day we're going to enter the fullness of God's heavenly Kingdom and see in front of us a tapestry where we will comprehend the root reason for everything. We will see the display of God's wisdom throughout the whole of human history from the beginning to the end and every thread of that great tapestry will display the unfathomable glory of God.

We will learn anew that everything and everyone is interconnected. That the human race is one people from a single common ancestor throughout all of human history. And what that means at a much smaller level for your family is that right now, as you read this, God is telling a story about His glorious nature through your family. And you and your immediate family are one chapter of that story. You didn't start the book and you're probably not going to end the book. What happens in your lifetime was greatly impacted (but not determined) by your parents and what will happen to your children, grandchildren and great grandchildren will be greatly impacted (but not determined) by you. God chose to do this first and foremost because it better displays His glory than to have created the world for one generation and then to end the story there.

You don't exist because God needed one more individual story to tell; you exist because you are part of a larger story where God is the main character and your family line is a supporting character. As Donald Miller put it, "I'm a tree in a story about a forest." So when you and your family make the decision to hate God and go to war against Him, the story of your family will likely lift up the glorious character of God's strength and when, by God's grace, your family trusts God and believes the Gospel, you become a glorious expression of His mercy. This doesn't mean individuals aren't free or aren't important. Questions of justice and specific sentences for individual wrongs are always assessed at the individual level (see Ezekiel 18), but it does mean family and family lines are far more important than the philosophers of the western project care to admit.

As you might imagine, realizing that God is telling a story through your family is going to have a huge impact on how you choose to build, lead and teach your family. And so the Bible gives us a vivid example of what one father did when he deeply understood the implications of this reality.

Passing on Generational Blessings

"...you will be called Abraham, for you will be the father of many nations. I will make you extremely fruitful. Your descendants will become many nations, and kings will be among them! I will confirm my covenant with you and your descendants after you, from generation to generation. This is the everlasting covenant: I will always be your God and the God of your descendants after you. And I will give the entire land of Canaan, where you now live as a foreigner, to you and your

descendants. It will be their possession forever, and I will be their God." **Genesis 17:5-8**

If you told a typical western man, "All that you do in your life, your money, your friendships and your favor with God is yours alone. Your children will have to make their own way in the world and you won't be able to pass these things on to them," many of them would be fine with this arrangement. It would seem fair. "We had to make our way and our kids will have to make their way. It's good for them." We might say to ourselves, "They need to learn that nothing comes free in this world." Then we'd get on with living our life and toward the end of it we might slap the popular "We're Spending Our Kids Inheritance" bumper sticker on our RV as we drive into the sunset to enjoy our golden years.

But if you told Abraham that all the resources, relationships and blessings he was building up during his lifetime could only be enjoyed by him alone, he would see this as terribly unfair and demotivating. Why the difference? What changed? Western people tend to think about fairness from the perspective of the individual while Abraham would have seen it from the perspective of the multigenerational family. The question you and I must ask is: which game are we playing? What kind of world did God architect? Did He design a world in which our lives are entirely determined by our individual choices or is our experience in life largely determined by our family? As a friend of mine said recently, there's a reason therapists spend 80% of the time digging into your family of origin. And we're learning this goes beyond psychology and can even influence our biology. Modern science is just beginning to discover that decisions made by one generation can alter the DNA code passed on to the next generation in a new discipline called epigenetics.

Individualism is also a cherished doctrine in western public policy. It's important to be aware of the fact that, when the US founding fathers crafted the Constitution, they did not try to balance individual rights with family rights. They only articulated individual rights. The word "family" does not appear even one time in the Constitution. This has given rise to centuries of policies that leave out any consideration for multigenerational family design. It's why a child's individual, constitutional rights to privacy in seeking an abortion at age thirteen can trump even the right of the parents to be notified. Individual rights are important, but so are family rights and western cultures simply don't understand or appreciate the latter. Perhaps there's no issue in the United States where this philosophy is more clearly discussed then in the debate over the Death Tax. Politicians openly talk about their intention to engineer a more fair society for individuals by enforcing an enormous tax on a family's money, that had already been previously taxed, when it's being passed to the next generation.

This would have mystified a man like Abraham. He would see these examples of state-sponsored individualism as a departure from God's design. Abraham worked hard his whole life to bless his family line. And even though God tested Abraham to ensure He was number one in Abraham's heart, God blessed Abraham by blessing his family. This single decision by God, to honor Abraham's desire by choosing and blessing his descendants, has placed Abraham's family at the center of the redemptive story God is telling the world ever since.

Since we are going to have such an outsized influence on our kids, mothers and fathers must choose to live their lives to bless their descendants. Parents have a tremendous responsibility and they have far more power and influence over the future than western people care to admit.

- [Blog] <u>How to Bless your Children After you Die</u>

If you are reading the physical copy of this book you can find the links to the digging deeper resources at familyteams.com/FR.

Generational Connections in the New Testament

"For the unbelieving husband is made holy because of his wife, and the unbelieving wife is made holy because of her husband. Otherwise your children would be unclean, but as it is, they are holy." **-1 Corinthians 7:14**

"Wait, isn't this just Old Testament stuff that was replaced by the coming of Christ?" Most Christians live as if the New Testament ushered in this new age of individualism by allowing us to safely ignore the generational themes established in the Old Testament. Far from contradicting the Old Testament, the New Testament adds to and builds on the family themes of the Old Testament.

One example repeated in the Gospels and Acts is the idea of targeting whole households for salvation. It seems the primary target of evangelism in the book of Acts was not the individual but the household. We see this pattern beginning in Jesus' ministry through His command to His disciples in Luke 10 to find the "man of peace," which He describes as the head of a household. When Jesus reached out to Zacchaeus, He did not declare the salvation of Zacchaeus as an individual but instead the salvation of his house (Luke 19:9). As the Gospel spread, the first instance of Gentiles receiving the Good News and the Holy Spirit was not an individual but the entire household of Cornelius (Acts 11:14). Lydia's household

(Acts 16:15), the jailer's household (Acts 16:31) and the household of Crispus (Acts 18:8) were the initial converts and basis of operation for the Apostle Paul. Why is this a repeated theme in the New Testament and not today? Why are most of our outreach efforts aimed at individuals instead of households? It's not that our understanding of salvation is inconsistent with the Apostles but that our understanding of family has dramatically changed.

One of the least-discussed commands in the New Testament that feels like it was lifted right out of the Old Testament is Paul's instruction to care for the previous generation when he writes, "if a widow has children or grandchildren, these should learn first of all to put their religion into practice by caring for their own family and so repaying their parents and grandparents, for this is pleasing to God." (1 Timothy 5:4, emphasis added). When's the last time you heard a pastor ask people not to volunteer for ministry unless they first are properly caring for their elderly parents? Yet this is exactly what Paul tells Timothy to do.

Perhaps the strongest statement of generational connection was made when Paul answered a question posed by the Corinthians about whether a person married to an unbelieving spouse should get a divorce. His answer is startling. He says, "She should not divorce him. For the unbelieving husband is made holy because of his wife, and the unbelieving wife is made holy because of her husband. Otherwise your children would be unclean, but as it is, they are holy." Western theologians have been scratching their heads over this verse for centuries, but amidst all the confusion regarding how exactly to interpret this passage, one thing is crystal clear: a strong generational connection exists between parents and children.

TOOLS FOR BUILDING A MULTI-GENERATIONAL FAMILY

But how does this affect Christian families in the 21st century? Are there practical ways we can begin to reflect the true multigenerational nature of family in the midst of modern western cultures?

Pushing the Generational Reset Button

"you ask. 'Doesn't the child pay for the parent's sins?' No! For if the child does what is just and right and keeps my decrees, that child will surely live.'" **Ezekiel 18:19-20**

Some of you might be wondering, "How is it fair that God allows a child to be so deeply impacted by the sins of their parents? Can't we start fresh?" The Good News is that Jesus came to make all things new. He paid the penalty for our sins so each generation that turns to the Lord can be fully saved. "For the promise is for you and for your children and for all who are far off, everyone whom the Lord our God calls to himself...Save yourselves from this crooked generation." (Acts 2:39-40, emphasis added).

When Joshua wanted to encourage the leaders of the families of Israel to be careful in how they led their households in the Promised Land, he gave this word: "This is what the LORD, the God of Israel, says: 'Long ago your ancestors, including Terah the father of Abraham and Nahor, lived beyond the Euphrates River and worshiped other gods. But I took your father Abraham from the land beyond the Euphrates and led him throughout Canaan and gave him many descendants...'" (Joshua 24:2-3) Joshua's point is that even Abraham's father was an idol worshiper, and look how much God blessed Abraham's descendants! So while blessings chase after a thousand generations of those who are faithful to God, we also need to understand the grace God gladly pours out on a generation that chooses to start over, beginning by repenting of the sins of their forefathers.

Many of you represent an Isaac and Rebekah generation building on the godly legacy of the past while others represent Abraham and Sarah generations—the first in your family line to turn back to the Lord. We're going to explore practical ways of integrating grandparents into your family life for Isaac and Rebecca generations, but if that is not a healthy option for you, don't be discouraged! Abraham had no intention of integrating his father Terah into his family. God told him to get away from Terah and the legacy of idol worship he represented and to start fresh in a new land (Genesis 12:1).

The message of Abraham is that there is no limit to the amount of blessing one faithful generation can store up for their family. So if you're feeling called to start over and press the generational reset button and found a new family, then prepare yourself now, even if you're young, to become the kind of patriarch and matriarch your new family line needs by understanding the role you will one day play as parents, grandparents and perhaps even great-grandparents of a family faithful to the Father. Your descendants will be very blessed if you do.

Releasing Grandparents

"May you live to enjoy your grandchildren." - **Psalm 128:6**

One of the clearest pieces of evidence that exposes the dysfunction in the western philosophy of family is the way we think about grandparents and older people in general. In the Torah, a grandfather was called a patriarch and given a place of honor, leadership and great significance in the family. In contrast, today we idolize youth. Westerners often see life peaking at some point in their 20s and afterward experience a slow, steady decline in their perceived value as a person. All of this is a direct result of our philosophy of family. Because the family is unimportant, the elders of the family are unimportant.

In the Bible, a good, rich life looks like a grandfather and grandmother, full of years, being surrounded by their children's children and living to bless their descendants. A beautiful picture of this is painted in the closing chapters of Genesis, where Jacob sees his son Joseph with his own eyes. Chapter 48 is dedicated to the way Jacob passed on blessings to Joseph's sons: "Jacob blessed the boys that day with this blessing: 'The people of Israel will use your names when they give a blessing. They will say, "May God make you as prosperous as Ephraim and Manasseh."'" (Genesis 48:20).

If you have parents who are willing and able to bless your family, then we as the generation having children need to find ways of bringing that blessing into our family life.

One way our family is trying to do this is during our family Shabbat (Sabbath) dinner (we'll discuss this in detail in the section about family traditions). We dedicate every Shabbat to one side of our family, alternating weeks between the Pryor side and the Seely side. My parents and April's parents lay their hands on their descendants and the patriarch says this blessing over the sons: "May the Lord make you like Ephraim and Manesseh and give you the faith of Abraham, the heart of David and the righteousness of Christ as you build our family from generation to generation." Over the daughters the matriarch will say, "May the Lord make you like Sarah, Rebecca, Rachel and Leah and give you heart of Ruth, the faith of Mary and the righteousness of Christ as you build our family from generation to generation."

We sometimes ask our parents to prepare family stories that teach biblical truths to present to the family. We often invite aunts, uncles, and cousins to our Sabbath meals. It's our privilege to provide a platform around which the family gathers to learn from the wisdom of our wisest members. But more than anything else, we and our children are sinking our roots deeper into our family identity. We learn what it means to be in the Pryor line and in the Seely line, both the good and the bad. We hear stories of the generations that went before us, see pictures and internalize the memories and experiences of our historic family. We honor their lives and we acknowledge that we are their legacy.

This is a big part of what it means to be a grandparent. No one knows and loves the family line like the grandparent who knew and loved two or three generations before them and knows and loves the two or three generations after them. When a grandparent sits at the family table, they stand as the bridge spanning between five and seven generations of the family. We must give faithful, loving, godly grandparents a place to bless and build our family identity. Instead of treating our kids like a blank slate and sending them off into the world to find themselves, we give them a strong and stable foundation. Through good grandparenting, children should know and honor who they are and where they came from. This does not hinder children from being fully themselves; on the contrary, having a solid foundation and deep roots lets you grow much higher than having shallow roots and a forgotten history.

As Tolkien wrote in the Lord of the Rings:
"All that is gold does not glitter,
Not all those who wander are lost;

The old that is strong does not wither,
Deep roots are not reached by the frost."

And as I said above, if your parents cannot build into your family because they have been unfaithful to the family, please don't be discouraged. Instead, prepare yourself for the amazing experience of getting to be the first patriarch and matriarch of a new faithful family you are building for future generations.

TOOL #3 –
THE MIS-
SION OF THE
FAMILY

Families were created to accomplish a mission.

Why should families work together as a team instead of separately as individuals? Anytime a team gets together, it's understood that what they are about to attempt to accomplish would be impossible if everyone chose to function alone. In other cultures there persists a belief that teams are to be valued more than the individual, a sentiment expressed beautifully in the African proverb, "If you want to go fast, go alone. If you want to go far, go together."

We've created a society that promotes and celebrates the idea of individual achievement above the accomplishment of the team. This is understandable in one sense, because teams are temporary. People come and go from my team at work, sports teams trade individual players as free agents, and there is an explosion of freelance workers whose business brand is their own name. But what if, instead of joining a team temporarily for a task and then returning to your life as an individual, you started out your life as part of a team that was designed to work together from the day you were born until the day you die? The only thing that could justify living your entire life in this state would have to be a mission so important that it could be worthy of the attention of every family member for generations. We must try to understand this mission. The emergence of your family team depends on it.

The First Family Mission

*"God blessed them and said to them, "Be fruitful and increase in number; fill the earth and subdue it. Rule over the fish in the sea and the birds in the sky and over every living creature that moves on the ground." **Genesis 1:28***

Why are we here? What is the purpose of life? Discovering the answers to these all-important questions is the only way to live a life of meaning. But we must have divine revelation from the Designer of all life to help give us the answers. We can't discover why we were made in the first place without getting a glimpse into the purpose of our Creator at the moment of our creation. We see clues about that purpose in our ability to communicate, procreate, organize, rule and build deep meaningful relationships, but are these tools an end in themselves, or are they the means to fulfilling something greater? Fortunately for us, God knew we would need Him to answer our question "Why are we here?" directly, so when He decided to make human beings He blessed us, and the first words we heard in our newly formed ears were our purpose: "Be fruitful... multiply... subdue the earth... rule".

And in these important directives we discover the original mission of family. God did not speak this to an individual but to a couple. In addition, the command to multiply obviously can't be given to an individual, only to a man and a woman. Then God took the first man and woman and placed them in a garden to tend it, and to expand it. Being fruitful and multiplying are tools for subduing and ruling God's creation. Of course, when we get to the third chapter of Genesis, we learn that something went terribly wrong, something that now confuses the simplicity and clarity of our first mission. We'll look at the impact of this event called "The Fall" next, but for now let's try and understand the original purpose of the family's design.

Perhaps the easiest way to understand the meaning of our mission to "subdue the earth" is to say that families were designed to create order out of chaos. Adam and Eve lived in an island of order (called the Garden of Eden) in a sea of chaos (the rest of the Earth). The Earth was a wild wilderness but it had within it all the raw materials needed to organize and sculpt creation into a flourishing habitat for human beings and every other creature.

To this day, just about all of our work as humans is a collective attempt to bring order to creation. Garbage collectors bring order through waste disposal, teachers bring order through organizing and disseminating human knowledge, artists bring the order of beauty into the drab and ugly, computer programmers use code to create software to assist with our mission to subdue. When a mother brushes tangles out of her daughter's hair she is fulfilling our mission to bring order out of chaos. But since the Earth was cursed after Genesis 3, instead of the whole world looking like Eden, we each have to expend enormous efforts just to keep our island of order free from the invading forces of chaos. Countless men step onto their little patch of grass on Saturday morning armed with complex chemicals and ingenious inventions to beat back the invading forces of chaos from his little island of order. This is what we were made for—except it wasn't supposed to be this hard. However, the need for continuous effort makes sense of the design of the family. It takes a fruitful and multiplying family to increasingly create order out of chaos throughout the vast expanse of time. We need the diverse family roles, the diverse strengths of the family, and the power to reproduce if we hope to see any lasting success in taking, holding and expanding our islands of order on the Earth.

Families were also made to rule, something we first learned through our stewardship of creatures and other lower forms of organic life. Parents throughout the world often give their children a pet as an initial lesson in responsibility because we learn great wisdom when we care for organic life. And we were also meant to ultimately learn rulership when we form human societies. Our story begins in the book of Genesis in a garden, but it ends in the book of Revelation in a city. Cities are to people what gardens are to plants and animals. Cities are a place were human gifts can be organized and released on a much larger scale to enable the human family as a whole to make progress. It's the city and the development of government that has advanced us to the level where we can produce hospitals, universities, and businesses that achieve more than what any single immediate family could produce on their own.

When we turn the page from Genesis 1 to Genesis 2 and 3, we see that deeply satisfying work and the abundance it afforded created the perfect environment for human beings to walk with God. After a day of blessed work, Adam and Eve rested and walked with God in the cool of the day and they were also given a day of rest every week to enjoy their relationship with God and each other. Families must work to provide enough abundance so each family member and the family as a whole can freely, consistently and aggressively pursue God on both a daily and a weekly basis. But this is not easy today. And even though the purposes of subduing, ruling and walking with God all persist to this day, they were greatly frustrated when something went terribly wrong.

Family Survival East of Eden

"...the ground is cursed because of you. All your life you will struggle to scratch a living from it." **Genesis 3:17**

Life is hard, but it wasn't designed to be this hard. Death, weeds, sickness, natural disasters and endlessly maintaining everything we plant, build or use are the results of the Fall in the Garden. Now we toil. Toil involves doing either more or different work than your capacity and talents were originally designed to do. And the consequences of our first father Adam's sin in the garden have been passed down from father to child so that the whole family—the whole human race—is infected. The result of this event for families is that, before we get to pursue all the wonderful purposes for which we were created, we must overcome and always stay one step ahead of the destroying forces that were unleashed when all of creation was cursed by our sin. Families were not originally created to toil just to scrape by, but now that we all live on the east side of Eden, toil is a constant part of our lives. Gaining an upper hand on the invading forces of chaos is a basic prerequisite to having the ability to following a greater vision.

Providing for a family after the Fall is hard work. And the command to provide is not just something we hear from the Old Testament. Paul tells Timothy to tell those who will not provide for the needs of their family that they have "denied the faith" and are "worse than an unbeliever" (1 Timothy 5:8). What faith have they denied? They are denying their faith in the Story spelled out in the Old Testament Hebrew Scriptures.

Some in the Church tend to think the New Testament encourages a reduced focus on our families in order to build and expand the Kingdom. We know Peter, James and John all left their family businesses to follow Jesus.

Here we encounter another important clarification between the single life and the married life. Single men and women are commanded to be fully devoted to the Lord (1 Corinthians 7:32); but Paul also makes it clear that those with spouses and children have divided interests and must tend to their "earthly responsibilities" (1 Corinthians 7:34). So anyone who fails to provide for their family denies the responsibilities laid upon mankind after the Fall.

Men especially must accept these circumstances and bear up under the weight of our call to first provide for our family. The curse to toil was specifically laid on men, not women (Genesis 3:17). Like it or not guys, we're called to scratch a living from this cursed earth. So let's get scratching.

The good news is that, while we toil, God continues to help us provide for the needs of our family. Often God will pour out blessing on our work which can, in turn, allow us to give more and more attention to fulfilling the global mission given to our families. Work existed before the Fall but toil did not and so we need to become skilled at directing our toilsome work in the wisest possible way so that our families need to toil less and we are released to work more in the areas of our calling, skills and passions.

Families and the Great Commission

"Dear friend, you are being faithful to God when you care for the traveling teachers who pass through" **3 John 5**

If God sent us out to rule and subdue the Earth, then how can we ever hope to accomplish this mission after our fall tainted all of creation with sin? And praise God, we do have salvation through the death and resurrection of Christ! But that salvation has not been brought back to all of creation. The earth is saturated with sin and in order to fulfill our first commission, to subdue the Earth, we have to return creation to a state of trust to our Creator. What is the point of creating order out of chaos if that order is setting up a rebellious regime designed to replace God?

This is why Jesus added a new commission to our original mission. Jesus told us to go and make disciples of all nations beginning with baptism, which declares the new disciple's surrender (or death) to their old, rebellious, independent life and delineates the entrance point into their new resurrected life. But the real work of the disciple-making process is summed up by Jesus' command to "teach them to obey everything I have commanded you." This is the mission of every disciple.

During Jesus' life He modeled the disciple-making process as a single man training single men, but how does a family make disciples? Should husbands leave their wives and children to fend for themselves while they travel the countryside teaching a band of followers? Many pastors and missionaries, deeply confused on this point, have essentially done just that. Most believers have never discovered the incredibly practical direction the New Testament gives to families on how to do their part in fulfilling the Great Commission, which looks very different than the disciple-making lifestyle of single men and women (1 Corinthians 7:34).

Our first detailed encounter with families participating in the disciple-making process in the New Testament is found in Luke 10, when Jesus sent 72 of his disciples into the mission field with a laser focus toward finding what he called "a man of peace". Jesus was so intent that they find this man that He told them not to greet anyone on the road and to immediately leave any village where a man of peace could not be found. A man of peace was someone with a house big enough to accommodate the traveling disciples, the ability to provide regular meals to feed them, and a reputation and network that could provide a platform for their ministry. In other words, the man of peace was the head of a strategic family in the village or city. Nowhere do we get the impression that the men of peace were told to leave their families and travel with the disciples. On the contrary, finding men of peace was critical because their consistent and stable lives allowed the message of the Kingdom spread among their communities.

This means that one of the best ways for families to participate in the Great Commission is to make their home a hub for a disciple-making ministry in their city or region. In fact, singles living a life fully devoted to the Lord often travel as they follow the leading of the Holy Spirit. If they want their ministry in a particular city to last and bear fruit over the long term, then they need to minister through a rooted, disciple-making family in each place they visit. Paul modeled this repeatedly in Acts (Cornelius in Acts 11:14, Lydia in Acts 16:15, the Philippian jailer in Acts 16:31, Crispus in Acts 18:8). When traveling equippers, single disciples and spiritual orphans throughout your city recognize your family as the hub for reproducing disciples then your family is what the New Testament referred to as an oikos, translated as house or household. One of the clearest and most important expressions of the Church in any city is the disciple-making rhythms of a believing household led by a man of peace.

Digging Deeper

- [Blueprint] Re-Church
- [Blog] Summary of N.T. Scholar Roger Gehring understanding of Oikos

If you are reading the physical copy of this book you can find the links to the digging deeper resources at familyteams.com/FR.

A Unique Family Vision

"For we are God's masterpiece. He has created us anew in Christ Jesus, so we can do the good things he planned for us long ago." - **Ephesians 2:10**

Once we have a clear understanding of our mission as families, we then need to consider how God may give a unique vision specifically to our family and our family line. The Old Testament has many examples of families who have unique callings that get passed down from generation to generation: Aaron's family was set aside for priestly ministry, David's family was set apart to rule, and the Korahites were gatekeepers (1 Chronicles 9:19), singers (2 Chronicles 20:19) and poets for hundreds of years who penned eleven of the Psalms. The narratives in the New Testament were largely written in one generation so it's difficult to see multigenerational ministry, but we do see some families beginning to take on special callings. Philip had four daughters who all prophesied (Acts 21:9), and Priscilla and Aquila seemed to have a foundation-laying ministry, traveling as a family and greatly helping Apollos in Ephesus better understand the Gospel (Acts 18:26), and later had a foundational ministry in Rome (Romans 16:3-5).

The concept of a family vision can be short-term, something you feel called to for a season; long-term, something you feel called to for life; or multigenerational, something your children and grandchildren feel called to. The longer the scope of the vision, the more important it is to allow God to place the calling on your kids' hearts. A calling may span generations by going to just one or a small number of your children while the others receive different callings which the family must also affirm and support. It's generally helpful for parents to begin to craft at least a short-term description of their vision to give their efforts focus and to communicate to their family and their community the direction they feel God is leading them. As you walk more into your seasonal vision, God will often begin to show you if the scope is bigger than what you originally conceived.

The New Testament talks a lot about spiritual gifts, a topic far too big to cover here, but spiritual gifts are a great indication of the direction God is leading your family. Your family can also clarify its vision by answering the remaining questions of who, where, how and why. Sometimes God gives families greater clarity on who. For example, some families believe they have a unique calling to orphans, widows, prisoners, the poor or some other specific group. Sometimes God begins to answer the question where by giving families a strong passion for a particular neighborhood, city, foreign city or country. Foreign ministry callings often naturally span generations as their children get the advantage of learning the culture or language of a place and are given a unique opportunity to bear fruit in that place. Some families gain clarity on how. The how may be through music, through teaching, through writing, through traveling, through counseling or some other means. Still others gain clarity on why. Some family missions centered on the why include standing against abortion because it is bringing a country under divine judgment, interceding for Israel because of its importance as a sign post during this time in history or raising money for families adopting children as a sign of the Gospel.

One of the great temptations we've noticed is when families allow their unique vision to completely eclipse the biblical family mission. We are called to be fruitful, multiply, subdue, rule, and make disciples. These callings are given to families in general and must be accomplished regardless of our unique callings. The New Testament is clear that everyone is called to make disciples and everyone is given a spiritual gift (or gifts), which means we all have the same general ministry (disciple-making) and we each have a special ministry (our spiritual gifts). We must do both. Yes, they may overlap, which is great. If your gift is to teach, that greatly overlaps with a calling to make disciples; but at any point if someone were to ask how your family's ministry is making disciples you must be able to draw a direct line between the ministry efforts of your family and specific disciples who are growing and reproducing.

Nothing brings a family team together like a family vision. Teams cannot and will not work well together, sacrifice for one another and push through major challenges without a clear vision. The way you craft and communicate the vision will be a big part of whether it gives energy and clarity to your family. Some families have gotten their vision down to a single sentence: "Our family trains disciples, grows the body, and releases the five-fold ministry." Others have crafted a vivid story of what their family will look ten years from now as they are flourishing in their calling. Don't put too much pressure on yourself to lay out the vision for your whole life (or especially your descendants) the first time you sit down to discern your calling. A vision is always a work in progress, and God is sovereign over how much He may choose to reveal to you at any given time. But whatever you do write out, communicate it as clearly as you can to your family. As you do, your family will begin to tell a story through your focused life together that will first amaze and then transform the world.

Digging Deeper

- [Book] <u>A Million Miles in a Thousand Years</u>: How I Learned to Live a Better Story by Donald Miller. Miller gives some vivid examples of family vision especially chapter 9 "How Jason Saved his Family"

If you are reading the physical copy of this book you can find the links to the digging deeper resources at <u>familyteams.com/FR</u>.

The Hidden Purpose of Family

"Now we see things imperfectly as in a cloudy mirror, but then we will see everything with perfect clarity." **1 Corinthians 13:12**

Most people seem to assume that God invented the idea of family around the same time He created the Earth, as a clever strategy for population expansion. But the Bible presents a very different reason for the creation of the family structure:

that there is something about the family that reflects the eternal nature of the Triune God. We see this in the very first chapter of Genesis, when God says to Himself, "Let us make human beings in our image, to be like us... male and female he created them." (Genesis 1:26-27). There is some mystery about male and female that shows us what God is like.

Then in the New Testament, when the Messiah comes onto the scene, he shocks the world by calling God his Father. "Jesus replied, 'My Father is always working, and so am I.' So the Jewish leaders tried all the harder to find a way to kill him. For...he called God his Father..." (John 5:17). Jesus' earthly identity was so completely eclipsed by his identity as a son of God that, at only twelve years old, Jesus loses contact with his earthly family during a pilgrimage to Jerusalem. When his parents finally find Him days later, He says, "Didn't you know I had to be in my Father's house?" (Luke 2:49). Jesus has many identities in the New Testament—savior, shepherd, friend, king—but the one He uses to refer to Himself more than any other is son. He shared this identity with His disciples when He taught them to address God as "our Father" (Matthew 6:9).

One of the most mind-blowing surprises in the New Testament was when Paul revealed the hidden purpose behind marriage. While writing general instructions about marriage to the church in Ephesus, Paul says, as almost a side comment, "[Marriage] is a great mystery, but it is an illustration of the way Christ and the church are one." (Ephesians 5:32). Wow! Now we know the root reason marriage exists. Marriage and family rise far above our immediate needs and desires—and even beyond our needs as the human race—and finds its ultimate purpose and source in the story of God Himself. As history continues and God pulls back the curtain on more of the mysteries about life, we can deepen our understanding of the ways marriage, family and many other basic elements of life are not human inventions or mere practical tools but living portraits displaying God's nature. He's telling us about Himself.

These hidden purposes behind fatherhood, sonship and marriage are very practical for those who place deep faith in their significance. I can't think of a better reason to get married and have children than to understand more deeply how God loves us like a parent or how Christ loves us like a spouse. We are all on a journey back to a deep, intimate relationship with God, and even on this side of Eden, God has given us vivid pictures in the design of Creation that reveal His heart for us. This is why Christians must refuse to go along with cultural redefinitions of family. Earthly expressions of father, mother, wife, husband, son and daughter were created to reflect greater spiritual realities. They are vivid, high-definition portraits showing us who God is. Every time I love my children, I'm teaching them and discovering for myself aspects of God's nature and His heart both for them and for me. Every time I choose to love my wife, I'm presenting to her and to the world a picture of the covenant-keeping love of Jesus Christ.

TOOLS FOR BEING A FAMILY ON MISSION

Families in today's culture, even in the church, are largely sitting on the sidelines. Church leaders call individuals into mission, but very few understand how to activate whole families, making the family the most underutilized resource in the western church. A pastor I worked under years ago used to tell me that when a couple began to have kids, they would basically kiss them goodbye as contributing members of the congregation for the next 10-15 years until their youngest was in school. Then maybe they might slowly begin to re-engage. We can reverse this pattern by understanding how the family can engage in mission together.

Becoming a Fruitful, Multiplying Family

"I chose you and appointed you that you should go and bear fruit, and that your fruit should remain..." **John 15:18**

Western families have an accounting problem. They tend to only count as significant those things they personally achieve in the productive years of their life. They have little to no vision for what happens 50 or 500 years after they die. Imagine if Abraham didn't care about whether or not he had children. In that one act of having Isaac, Abraham blessed the world with Moses, David, Jesus and all of the apostles—in fact the entire Jewish race. If you were to assess the fruit of Abraham's life, what percentage of his fruitfulness was achieved by all the work he did during his life compared with what he accomplished through the act of having and raising Isaac? The comparison is almost absurd. Virtually all his fruitfulness came through Isaac. We wouldn't even have the stories of Abraham's life without Isaac.

When western people read about Abraham's passion for descendants, we tend to dismiss this desire as primitive. I read the stories about Abraham in Genesis for many years in order to learn from Abraham's faith, but it never occurred to me to learn fruitfulness from Abraham. But let's face it, when we compare our fruitfulness to Abraham's, we need to admit that we may be the primitive ones. We gratify momentary desires while sacrificing the opportunity to multiply our influence into the far distant future. We have, in Abraham, the ultimate example of productivity. Decisions Abraham made almost 5000 years ago are still shaping world events today. Just pick up a newspaper and count the articles that can be traced back, in some way, to father Abraham.

The problem with our accounting is that we don't respect the power of multiplication. When God told us to be fruitful and multiply, he was showing us that these concepts are inextricably linked to one another. One way you become fruitful is by multiplying. And not just in the area of having children but in every area of life. Multiplication is a key component to lasting fruitfulness.

Let's take work as another example. Imagine what would happen if someone chose to exchange working 40 hours per week on one-time tasks with working a few hours per week on a system that multiplies. That person's productivity over time would explode exponentially. This isn't even a matter of opinion—it's simply a mathematical fact, yet we continue to focus our greatest efforts toward short-term, one-time gains. Why? The answer is actually fairly simple. Like we noted before, western people believe in the supreme value of the individual and so when the individual dies, their continued productivity ceases to matter since they are not alive to enjoy the fruits of their individual achievements. It's only when you believe in the value of family and see the family as a multigenerational line that you begin to value multiplication as the pathway to family fruitfulness.

How many activities in your typical week are focused on multiplication? Family activities like having children, adopting children, training children and grandchildren, developing repeatable family traditions all have the ability to multiply if done well, and can outlive you by many centuries.

Getting our families back on our original mission to be fruitful and multiply begins by following in the footsteps of our father Abraham and committing to bear fruit that multiplies. Fruit that will remain.

Becoming a Subduing, Ruling Family

"...whoever wants to become great among you must be your servant, and whoever wants to be first must be slave of all." - Mark 10:43-44

I'm often asked how to write a family mission statement. But remember, family was God's idea, and family already comes preloaded with a mission statement. In Genesis 1, we read that God created the first family and gave them a two-part mission. We already discussed the first, being fruitful and multiplying; the second part was to rule. Humans were to fill the Earth and subdue it by ruling over God's creation as stewards.

Did you know families were created to rule? But like everything else, this purpose was complicated and greatly altered by the Fall. Jesus taught us that the purpose of having power is to provide a greater platform for serving others, which can be learned and then expressed through the family.

Strong, godly families in Christ's Kingdom should not shy away from increasing their influence in the world. But how and why we gain and use that influence should be completely different than the pattern of this world. If you are not prepared to steward this power correctly, then please don't seek it. The taint of the Fall is deep within us, and power very often brings out the worst in people. But families will quickly gain a lot of ground when they simply steward the gifts and talents of each family member in a coordinated way over time.

God created human beings with all the necessary tools to rule, and we are still the only stewards this world has. If we abdicate our responsibilities, the world will descend into chaos. Fields need farmers, animals need ranchers, businesses need owners, students need teachers, governments need leaders and the church needs elders. We have a lot of ruling and subduing yet to do, and if your family does not prepare its members to take up these positions and serve, then others, possibly with very different motives, will.

But as many traps and landmines as there are in this topic of influence, power and servant leadership, the family is uniquely designed to help us successfully navigate through this maze to the other side.

First, families are an ideal environment to learn servant leadership. The family setting challenges us almost every moment of the day to put aside our own selfish interests and help others who are often younger, weaker and more vulnerable. Compare this to individuals who grew up in an environment designed entirely to serve them. This is the case for many in our society today, and these individuals are far less prepared to lead. Strong families can also keep members in check once a leadership position is gained. Who can speak truth to power better than a member of your own family who you know loves you and is loyal to you?

One of the greatest reasons multigenerational families should serve in positions of influence is because they care the most about the long-term implications of critical societal decisions. An example that countries throughout the world are dealing with today is the decision of one generation to intentionally saddle the next generation with crushing debt while they live off the benefits of their children's credit. Every time a government thoughtlessly runs enormous deficits that they know future generations will be unable to pay back, they are committing generational theft. But because politicians are often professionals who rarely intentionally build a multigenerational family, they care little about the consequences of these actions.

In the past, villages, cities and countries were led by a group of elders who were the heads of the strongest multigenerational families in the region. They could be trusted, more than other fallen humans, to make wise decisions for their communities because their children and grandchildren would be the ones forced to live with the consequences of their decisions. And because their lives were quickly coming to a close, they would make decisions that would serve the coming generations. Today's systems of government have shifted away from relying on wise grandfathers to relying on young professional, career-driven, lifelong politicians who use polls to determine their position on most issues.

Grandparents, we need your help. When your children move out of your home and begin to have children of their own, when you retire from regular work or pass on your business assets and your free time increases, that is the moment we need you to serve the greater community. Please don't head to a retirement community and leave us to be led by self-serving politicians. We need you in leadership. Your children's and your children's children's quality of life will largely depend on whether or not you choose to serve.

Becoming a Beautiful Family

"And we all, who with unveiled faces contemplate the Lord's glory, are being transformed into his image with ever-increasing glory, which comes from the Lord, who is the Spirit."
-2 Corinthians 3:18

We discovered there is a hidden purpose for family. We as families actually get to reflect elements of God's divine nature, a reflective portrait that can be either ugly or beautiful. When someone says, "You have a beautiful family," what do they really mean? People can't authentically say this about a family that is physically beautiful but full of abuse and turmoil or that is raising children to be spoiled.

Beauty is really the result of everything being so strikingly balanced and in order that it touches your heart. It triggers a memory in your spirit of the way things are actually meant to be. All beauty is the discovery of something that reflects God's original design in a surprisingly clear way. A beautiful family is like shock therapy for the world. It wakes us up, gives us hope and awakens a longing for God and his Kingdom. That is why becoming a beautiful family is an essential part of our mission. Mission is not just about what we do but who we are. It's not about simply reacting to the Fall but reflecting the glory of God's original design. Families on this side of Eden will never do that perfectly. Every family has problems and every family will go through serious seasons of internal struggle. But we need to see building beautiful family as a part of our mission. The world needs to see loving families.

For too long, families have been perceived as a barrier to mission instead of a conduit for mission. Some missionaries still send their children to boarding schools, while pastors hide their families and family problems from public view. The family is not the place you go to retreat from mission—it's the community through which you go on mission. A beautiful family is a missional community.

We just returned from spending two and half months in Jerusalem with our five kids, and our kids were absolutely indispensable in opening doors and hearts to the truth of the Gospel. And it wasn't primarily any individual child; it was the family dynamic that seemed to make the difference. That's why, in this next section, we need to explore one of the primary tools for building a beautiful family: the diverse roles of the family.

TOOL #4 - THE ROLES OF THE FAMILY

Families have a well-crafted, God-given design and structure that gives the family team all the diverse parts it needs to work together in harmony in order to accomplish its mission

Nothing seems to stir up controversy in western culture quite like discussing predefined roles. "What right does society have to define for us who we are or what we should do?" we ask. And to our culture's credit, society doesn't have that right. There is only one good reason to allow someone else to define your identity and purpose and that is if that someone was the One who created you in the first place. The Architect of our lives knows why He made our muscles, our emotions, our instincts, our anatomy, our life cycle the way He did. And if there is real purpose behind this design, then it pre-defines our lives. Fighting it is to be at war with ourselves.

A Harvard professor of gender studies was expressing her frustration with the way the western cultural elite, in claiming that gender differences are only the result of societal conditioning, actively tries to suppress obvious scientific data that contradicts their ideology. She then told the story of a highly educated couple who were determined not to allow their daughter to be infected by societal attempts to define her as a girl. One Christmas, their little girl opened her presents and discovered, to her delight, a couple of toy construction trucks. Bursting with excitement she immediately ran upstairs. After a few minutes her parents went to check on her and when they knocked at her bedroom door, she opened it just a crack and said, "Shhhhh, they're asleep." To their great surprise, like a good mommy, their daughter had carefully put the trucks to bed.

Try as we might to deny that a master design exists, this design inconveniently rears its head in spite of our best attempts to repress it. The fact is, men and women are very different, and we differ for some very important reasons that find their purpose in the way God designed the family.

THE BIBLE'S DESCRIPTION OF FAMILY ROLES

"My son, obey your father's commands, and don't neglect your mother's instruction." **Proverbs 6:20**

As Tolstoy famously wrote in Anna Karenina, "All happy families resemble one another; each unhappy family is unhappy in its own way." Like anything that was designed for a specific purpose, there's a particular pattern families were created to follow... and countless alternative patterns that simply don't work. This doesn't mean families cannot have their own distinctives, but you'll be far more successful at diversity if you first understand the purpose and intended function of the family design so you can work with and through that design rather than fighting it. As in every other area of life: if all else fails, read the instructions. God has not left us wandering in the dark. He has given us vivid descriptions of each of these roles; we need to understand them, accept them and teach them to others.

The Role of the Father

"He must manage his own household well, with all dignity..." **1 Timothy 3:4**

Biologists who study human birth have outlined over 20 instantaneous physiological changes that occur within the body of every baby the moment they take their first breath. Multiple systems come online for the first time to prepare the newborn to survive in the outside world. But there's another equally amazing and important metamorphosis happening nearby that will prove every bit as crucial for future survival as a healthy respiratory system: a man just became a father. I vividly remember the moment this happened to me and I was unprepared for its sweeping impact on every part of my life. I suddenly saw the whole world differently. It was as if I understood for the first time the true purpose of my masculinity. I felt compelled to go out and use all of my might to shape a world worthy of this God-given gift: my precious, baby girl. My daughter.

While mothers experience vulnerability after the birth of their newborn and retreat into the protective environment of the home to care for and nurture this new, helpless, little life, fathers very quickly go on the offensive.

As you read through the Bible to get help in understanding this new role, you won't find much useful insight from our first father Adam. His legacy seems to be largely as a passive husband and absent father. Noah protected his family from the flood but died shortly after cursing his grandson in the midst of an epic hangover. But when we arrive at Abram (Hebrew for "exalted father), who became Abraham (Hebrew for "father of many nations), we find a man who, while fallen in his own way, truly understood the design of fatherhood. The entire narrative of Abraham's life is a practical outline, in story form, for how to be a wise, effective father. Every father would be blessed by studying the pattern Abraham has set for fatherhood. Here's a brief snapshot of what Abraham did as our prototypical father.

- Genesis 12 - Trusting God: Abram's radical trust in God provides a divine, multigenerational blessing for his future family.
- Genesis 13 - Family Alliances: Abram's assets and investments greatly multiply and he secures a lasting peace and powerful alliance with Lot's family by creating clear land boundaries.

- Genesis 14 - Household training: Abram's trained warriors protect the family by rescuing Lot and a number of regional kings from an invading force.
- Genesis 15 - Family Covenant: God promises Abram descendants, makes a covenant with Abram, and Abram's faith in the covenant is credited to him as righteousness.
- Genesis 16 - Doubt and Temptation: Abram stumbles trying to fulfill God's promise through Sarai's servant Hagar and has Ishmael.
- Genesis 17 - Family Identity: God changes Abram's name to Abraham, the father of many nations, and gives him the covenant of circumcision, cutting the sign of the covenant into the skin for all future generations of his family.
- Genesis 18-19 - Family Intercession: God visits Abraham and Sarah; Abraham negotiates with God on behalf of his nephew Lot and his family in Sodom.
- Genesis 20 - God's Faithfulness: Abraham calls Sarah his sister and God intervenes to protect Sarah when she is given to the king Abimelek
- Genesis 21 - Family Conflict: Abraham sends Ishmael away to reduce family rivalry and makes a treaty with Abimelek and negotiates for water rights for his family.
- Genesis 22 - Gospel Faith: Abraham is tested and proves to God that his heart belongs fully to the Lord through the sacrifice of Isaac.
- Genesis 23 - Family Memorials: Abraham secures a burial plot for his family and carefully records the transaction details for future generations.
- Genesis 24 - Spouse Finding: Abraham gets just the right wife for his son Isaac.
- Genesis 25 - Succession Planning: Abraham passes all the blessings, promises and assets he had

accumulated during his life to his son Isaac and then, surrounded by his family, he dies.

Can you see who a father is and what a father does through Abraham? Fatherhood is a fairly simple idea. Fathers live to bless their future generations, so wisdom for a new father largely consists of choosing to spend the rest of his life serving his grand- and great-grandchildren. Building a strong, God-honoring, abundant, multigenerational family was the job you received the moment your first child was born. Following the leading of the Holy Spirit, making covenants with God, trusting in the promises of Christ, multiplying assets, securing family alliances, training to protect and defend friends and family, setting clear, legally binding land boundaries and water rights, having and training children, establishing a family burial plot, finding great spouses for your children and ensuring everything you've built is passed down in a safe way to the next generation is your to-do list before you die. Dads, let's get to work.

The Role of the Mother

"Never! Can a mother forget her nursing child?
Can she feel no love for the child she has borne?" -Isaiah 49:15

Motherhood is taking a beating. According to Pew Research, the number of women in their 40s who have never had a child has doubled since the 1970s. No single role has suffered from more confusion because of the western idea of family than the role of the mother. Restoring the family as a team has the power to elevate motherhood once again.

It's important to acknowledge that seeing family as merely a collection of individuals instead of a team will often leave mothers holding the short end of the stick. While everyone else feels entitled to put their individual needs above the family, mothers are forced to sacrifice their bodies to bear the children, are expected to sacrifice their work to care for their new infant, and often feel the most guilty when the needs of their children aren't being properly met. Given this unfair state of the western family, it's no surprise women are opting out.

But when everyone in the family sees the family as their primary team, women find motherhood far less isolating and much more fulfilling. So what might this look like?

It's time to look at Proverbs 31 with fresh eyes. This chapter describes, in poetic form, the ways of the virtuous mother at the peak of her power. This is not a checklist of things to accomplish but an aspirational ideal.

Proverbs 31 is one of the most misunderstood chapters in the entire Bible. Almost no chapter so clearly expresses what life looks like as a classical family, but western Christians tend to read our western context into the chapter. Instead of seeing a well-organized COO at the head of a series of flourishing entities, they see a lone mother who works herself to death. Let's look at the outline of elements that went into her role as mother.

- vs. 11-12. Her husband trusts her and she brings him good not harm. A woman was designed to work closely with her husband and help him execute the family vision with loyalty to the family and great skill.
- vs. 13, 19, 21, 22 - She goes beyond ensuring her family is warm while bringing beauty into the everyday things of life.
- vs. 14 - She has great taste and ensures her family eats a nutritious, diverse and delicious diet.
- vs. 15 - She assigns duties to the household helpers

(these can be children, domestic help or family business employees).

- vs. 16 - She's an astute investor, expanding and maximizing the family resources along with her husband.
- vs. 17-18 - She's a passionate, hard worker.
- vs. 20 - She leads the family in providing assistance and services to the poor.
- vs. 23 - Because the family is so well managed, her husband can serve the city as an elder.
- vs. 24 - When the family's productivity surpasses what the family needs, she sells the excess to produce an additional revenue stream.
- vs. 25 - Her temperament is joy and confidence. She walks with great dignity, and as she looks into the future, she laughs knowing her family is secure.
- vs. 26 - She teaches and trains others.
- vs. 27 - She runs a tight ship through constant evaluation and the use of discipline when needed.
- vs. 28-31 - She amazes and delights her children and her husband, who praise her to others knowing that she is a tremendous, God-given blessing to the family.

It's important to understand that this woman is a model to give women a very high bar for which to strive, not to make women feel like a failure. If you aim at nothing you tend to hit it and so we have here a way of finding areas of growth and improvement. It's also important to note that this woman was probably apprenticed to her mother, who spent decades modeling these things for her, and that she is now most likely an older matriarch of a large, flourishing family team with lots of resources to help her get things done. We live in a very different time and things won't look exactly like this, but the role outlined her is still very instructive to women today.

The Role of the Son

"unto us a son is given." -Isaiah 9:6

No family identity has been more perfectly modeled for us than what it means to be a son. Jesus Christ is the Ultimate Son. He emphasized many identities while on the Earth. He talked about Himself as the Good Shepherd, the Vine, and as the Messiah, but the most frequent title he used to describe himself was as a Son. And like so many of the other identities we're exploring, this one has been largely redefined in the west.

Throughout history, in every classical culture, there existed the idea of a good son. At a young age, male children who had strong families and loving parents would usually be very motivated to fill this role well. Sons would have a sense of their importance, knowing that many lives depended on their ability to grow in strength, wisdom and loyalty to the family. Since everyone in the household wanted the son to succeed in his development, everyone in the community played their part to reinforce the son's identity.

But no one had the power to help the son come into this role like the father. It was the father who, with a single word of praise, could forever settle for his child that he was indeed a good son. Likewise, a father, with very few words, could scar his son for life by making clear that he failed to measure up. God gave fathers the power to speak words directly into the identity of their sons because a man becomes a good son by following the vision and leadership of his father.

We can learn everything we need to know about being a good son (whether of our earthly father or, more importantly, of our heavenly Father) through specific things Jesus said and did. Let's walk through the way Jesus came into this identity as a son:

- Hebrews 10:4-7 - The son volunteers to go on the father's rescue mission
- Luke 2:8-21 - The father throws a huge party at the birth of his son
- Luke 2:41-50 - At the age of 12 while in Jerusalem Jesus' sonship identity totally eclipsed all his other identities
- Luke 2:51-52 - Through obedience to his earthly parents, Jesus grew in wisdom and favor learning how to be a good son
- Matthew 3:13-16 - Before Jesus begins his public ministry his father declares to the world that he loves and is pleased with his son.
- John 2:13-23 - Jesus defends the purity and purpose of his Father's house in his first clearing of the temple.
- John 5:19-20 - Jesus says He only does what He sees the Father doing.
- John 8:28-29 - Jesus only does what the Father taught him and is sent on a mission from the Father.
- John 10:30 - Jesus says He is one with the Father.
- Matthew 17:5 - Again, the Father publicly says he loves and is pleased with his son and that the disciples should listen to him.
- John 17 - The Father and the Son glorify each other, give authority back and forth to one another and intimately know each other.

Of course our earthly relationship with our father is only a dim reflection of God the Father's relationship with God the Son. All our experiences as earthly fathers and sons serve to prepare us for our sonship with our heavenly Father. That's why we as fathers and sons get to reflect many of these elements in our relationships with each other as we prepare to follow Jesus on the path toward loyal, lifelong sonship.

A son is the father in microcosm. Jesus tells the story of a man who sent many servants to a group of evil tenants to collect his due. After they beat and kill the servants, the father chooses to send his son saying, "They will respect my son." Western parents gasp at this decision but it's important to understand the father wasn't sending an individual—he was sending "the son". The son fully represented the will and authority of the father. Likewise, when Isaiah prophesied that a "son would be given," nothing could inspire more hope than for God to send His son. To classical families, the son is not a male individual but the embodiment of the future of the family with the full authority of the father.

Because sons get their identity from the father and will one day grow to embody his life and his will, sons and fathers must spend a great deal of time together. This begins with the father showing his sons everything he is doing and why. This continues through the father sending his sons on missions on behalf of the whole family. This culminates when the son takes the father's place as head of the family when his will rules, as he directs his sons, and the cycle continues in order to build up the family line into the future.

The Role of the Daughter

"I also know about everything you have done for your mother-in-law since the death of your husband...May the Lord, the God of Israel, under whose wings you have come to take refuge, reward you fully for what you have done." **- Ruth 2:11-12 (spoken by Boaz)**

In Christ, before our heavenly Father, we all receive the blessing of the firstborn son. Paul made this clear when he wrote, "[I]n Christ Jesus you are all sons of God, through faith. For as many of you as were baptized into Christ have put on Christ. There is neither Jew nor Greek, there is neither slave nor free, there is no male and female, for you are all one in Christ Jesus. (Galatians 3:26-29)" The Gospel is what makes this amazing miracle possible. We all relate to the Father through Jesus the firstborn son. We are positionally in Christ. None of us could ever stand before God from our natural position because of our sinfulness but when, through faith, we accept Christ's position, we eternally relate to the Father through this new location—in the Son. That is why Paul says we are the body of Christ. This is not just an analogy but a positional reality. Every Christian who is saved by Christ is in Christ making up his Body. Therefore, being in Christ, we are all sons of God. We are all treated as Christ is treated and we all, whether male or female, make up the body of the firstborn Son of God.

This makes the role of daughter a bit tricky on this side of the cross. There is a classical role of daughter described and celebrated in the Old Testament that is still very important and valid today. However, we also must train our daughters to come into their full spiritual inheritance and new position as part of the firstborn Son of their heavenly Father. So all the things described above about firstborn sons apply positionally to our daughters. However, in our earthly families, we still live out our unique roles, and daughters are especially designed and equipped to fill the daughter role.

In Scripture no one embodied the daughter role more beautifully than Ruth. This short story, publicly read by religious Jews to this day during the holiday of Shavuot (Pentecost), gives a great narrative depiction of how a daughter saved her mother-in-law and her husband's family line. It describes how her loyalty and sacrifice founded the dynasty of David and the line of the Messiah. Here are some of the daughter elements we learn from Ruth's story.

- Ruth 1:12 - Ruth was deeply concerned about her deceased husband's family line.
- Ruth 1:16-17 - Ruth rescued her family line by caring for her mother-in-law Naomi.
- Ruth 2:2 - During tough times Ruth worked hard and did whatever she could to support her family.
- Ruth 2:11-12 - Ruth left her parents' families and put her fate in the hands of her new family, coming under their protection and receiving their blessing.
- Ruth 3 - Ruth skillfully worked for the rights of her family, being both assertive and creative.
- Ruth 4:13-22 - Ruth bore children for the family and became the great grandmother of David.

Daughters are a continuous source of beauty, joy, productivity and loyalty within a family. Their role however, is the most internal to the family team. When the family is weak daughters can't find a place for their gifts within the family and often begin to follow a more traditionally male path outside the family or they seek to attach to a man from another family.

They are meant to get strength and identity from a loving father who adores them. But without that they will either compete for significance in ways traditionally done by men or they will find ways to attract the adoration of other men who may use them and seek to exploit their vulnerability.

Yes, daughters can and often should work as we see in the Ruth's example. A daughter will often surpass a son in productivity. But she's driven by something different. She wants to help. God has made her a helper, which means she loves to be inspired by a vision and to be included as a critical part of the team that makes things happen. Wouldn't it be wonderful if our families had a vision clear enough and worthy enough of the efforts of our daughters within our family teams?

Daughters are being chewed up by our society. An epidemic of eating disorders in numbers never before seen in history have emerged as daughters struggle to find their identity. But who's going to give that identity to them? It was designed to come first from a loving father and then be constantly affirmed by all the members of the family team.

Fathers must love their daughters with great affection and mothers must train their daughters to value and embrace humble service to others. A well-functioning family team with all the roles intact can make this happen for daughters, but the role of daughter, more than any other, depends on the other roles of the family to do their part so they can flourish within the family.

Summary of the Roles of the Family

One danger in clarifying roles is that people will define them so narrowly that they don't allow for creative exceptions. Please remember that these are generalizations. But generalizations are still very important, because without generalizations there is no wisdom. Wisdom comes from the ability to notice general patterns laid out by the architect of Creation, while also recognizing the wondrous diversity in His design as well. This should not stop us from describing general realities but we also must be cautious in judging ourselves or others. It's great to learn from generalizations but remember, there is only one you. We must balance celebrating design with celebrating uniqueness—one of the great things western society is trying to teach the world.

TOOLS FOR THE DIFFERENT ROLES WITHIN THE FAMILY

Bringing a Son into Manhood

"When I was a child, I talked like a child, I thought like a child, I reasoned like a child. When I became a man, I put the ways of childhood behind me." **1 Corinthians 13:11**

Boys must be initiated into manhood. They are born hearing a series of growing, gnawing, unrelenting questions that ask if they are good enough, strong enough, man enough... and if these questions are not answered with the help of the men in their lives, they will spend their lives trying to answer these questions on their own. Mature, thoughtful, wise cultures have always created clear pathways for boys to become men. So what does that say about western culture that it not only fails to provide this path but also deconstructs these paths faster than any of us can create them? We have an epidemic in our culture of the boy-man (boys in men's bodies), and it's getting worse.

In cultures with clear rites of passage into manhood, adolescence is an event that happens during testing period that lasts one to six months and often ends in a celebration ceremony. At that ceremony, the men who define masculinity in that boy's life—fathers, uncles, male family friends, grandfathers—welcome the boy into manhood and pledge to treat him, from that day forward, as a man. When those nagging questions arise, he can think back to how he handled the testing period, or he can remember the ceremony, or he can just look to the latest interaction with another man who treated him like a fully responsible man. That is how a culture gives men the ammunition they need to silence their nagging questions and enter fully into their male identity.

Men cannot do this on their own because identities are formed in community, not in isolation. For example, you can tell yourself you're a great artist every hour of every day, but the community must validate that claim for it to become a part of your identity. Those who have the ability to convince themselves of identities that no other objective person will affirm are narcissistic and antisocial. God designed us to receive certain things from others—especially from our families—and the family is responsible to provide and play our part in clarifying those identities.

The first step toward facilitating this transition to manhood is leaving childhood. Rites of passage should create some stark example where the person is clearly cut off from their previous environment to prepare for this transition. In Peter Pan this was the impending event of Wendy leaving the nursery. In the military, one of the first things they do is cut off the recruit's hair. Your old identity is falling away and making room for the coming of this new identity. Think about those things in your son's life that cause him to identify with childhood. Discuss with him what it looks like to leave those things behind. Put them in a box and give them away or hand them down to other children. He can change the clothes he wears, how he styles his hair, what he plays with, who he plays with, how he plays. This is a process of stripping away.

Now a quick word to western moms who are reading this and reacting with something between nostalgic sadness and horror at this process. Some mothers really struggle with this processes empathizing with their child. Imagine for a moment if in five years your family was going to be attacked by a ruthless enemy. Do you want your son, who has the strength to defend your family, to run away like a little boy from a battle he could have won, to save himself, while all the weaker members of the family are assaulted? Sorry to be so graphic, but it takes something like the quiet complacency of a suburban western lifestyle to grieve the transition of a boy becoming a man instead of celebrating it. Even if your son grows up in a safe corner of the western world, enemies will come from outside and from within to tear your family and his future family apart. It takes a man to face down the internal enemies of laziness, gluttony, selfishness, drunkenness and escapism as well as the external enemies of poverty, worldliness, criminals, injustice, failures and demonic doctrines. No matter how safe we feel at the moment, we all live in a real world with real dangers, and God designed men to stand on the front lines and face these dangers for their family.

Nothing hurts women more than immature men who run away when things get a little tough. We must learn to hate the Peter Pan fantasy of never growing up. Let your children experience a childhood full of wonder and play, and then rip them out of that world into adulthood as starkly and cleanly as each of us were suddenly removed from the safe, dark, warm world of the womb to face the cold, bright world. We do males, families, and this world no favors when we seek to prolong our son's childhood.

The next phase of transition involves a testing period. This phase may last for several months, where the boy experiences significant challenges, some that he may face with the help of other men and others that he must face alone. The challenges should be calibrated to build his confidence in how God has given him strength of body, mind and will.

The final phase is reintegration, where he comes back to the community, but as a different person. He now knows at a deeper level who he is and what he is capable of. But more than anything, he now knows why God has given him all the powers he possesses. During reintegration, his accomplishments during the phase of transition should be celebrated, recognized and affirmed, especially by the men in his life, as marks that he is indeed a man.

Once this pronouncement is clearly made, the family must treat him like a man. This does not mean, by the way, that he ceases to be a son. Unlike our western perception, where sonship is one stage of childhood, real sonship is entered into when the son of a family, with all of the power of manhood, submits those powers to a loving, wise father, who directs his sons to use their strength in strategic ways to protect and build the family. The further transition from sonship to fatherhood is yet another important rite of passage, but it should happen smoothly, along with all other transitions in a man's life, if he has fully moved from boyhood to manhood.

Digging Deeper

- [Article] Where Have All the Good Men Gone? Kay S. Hymowitz argues that too many men in their 20s are living in a new kind of extended adolescence.

If you are reading the physical copy of this book you can find the links to the digging deeper resources at familyteams.com/FR.

Women Training Women

"These older women must train the younger women to love their husbands and their children, to live wisely and be pure, to work in their homes, to do good, and to be submissive to their husbands." **Titus 2:4-5**

Women today need clear apprenticing more than ever. They don't know what it means to be a biblical woman and often have been discipled their whole lives to resist the concept of biblical womanhood.

The other day I saw a woman wearing a t-shirt that read, "Well-behaved women rarely make history." This slogan perfectly sums up the ethos of how women are encouraged in western societies today. They are taught to nurture a rebellious spirit of aggressive independence. They are taught they will be insignificant if they choose to spend their skills serving their family. But what will these kinds of messages do to the role of mothers? Feminist movements want to redefine the place of women in society as a whole but they often refuse to, at the same time, protect and build up the idea of motherhood. They see the primary struggle of women as a competition against men instead of seeing men and women working together as a team to build families and raise their children. The consequence of these kinds of messages have been devastating to our idea of motherhood. A society that does not honor motherhood will do great damage to the next generation.

What can we do against an idea that has gained so much ground in modern western culture? The answer is simple: older women must train younger women.

The church is full of mothers with adult children who have become confused about what to do next. They spent their lives developing their child-rearing and homemaking skills and assume it's now time to begin developing a career. While this may be a great path for some women, perhaps we should first consider Paul's clear command that older women train younger women from the wealth of experience they've spent decades acquiring. But because we are so isolated in western culture, many older women find it difficult to develop deep enough relationships with younger women to initiate this training. Meanwhile, younger women are assaulted with false messages about womanhood all day long while they attempt to fulfill in complete isolation a job for which they've never been trained. No wonder so many burn out and give up. The Bible's solution to this problem is older women stepping up and initiating a discipling relationship. Older women, please move out into your community and extend a hand to young wives and mothers. Initiate contact. We need this today more than ever.

The primary way "well-behaved" women make history is the same way well-behaved men make history: through their families. This statement is ironic, because if you look at most of the men and women who have made history, you will notice they were raised by a mother who chose to nurture them in a self-sacrificing way. Mothers, like fathers, make history all the time through their families. We need to celebrate the role wives and mothers play in the events that shape history. Perhaps then this modern myth will finally be exposed as a distortion that is working to unravel the foundation of our society.

Healing from Parental Wounds

"And he will turn the hearts of fathers to their children and the hearts of children to their fathers, lest I come and strike the land with a decree of utter destruction." - Malachi 4:6

According to psychologist Carl Jung, one of the clearest evidences for the existence of God was the existence of the same basic archetypes in the subconscious of every human being, regardless of their background or culture. And the strongest archetypes we all collectively share are for father and mother. God designed human beings with a need for a father and a mother, not just a male and female guardian. These roles were designed to play very specific parts in our development so that we can mature in a healthy way. The problem is, everyone who attempts to play the part of father or mother is bound to fall short in properly reflecting critical elements of those archetypes, leaving children with wounds. Various cultures deal with this problem in different ways. For a while in America, it was considered dishonorable to publicly talk about family issues and so several generations repressed their sense that something was really wrong and tried to ignore these issues. Then it became popular to blame our parents for every problem in our lives. But today there is a growing movement to bring much-needed balance to this issue, where we address wounds caused by inadequate parenting in order to experience healing in our relationship with God the ultimate Father.

We are all fallen and we are all damaging one another in both obvious and subtle ways. But the more we learn about and submit to God's design for fatherhood and motherhood, the more healthy our whole family will be.

A common wound many must overcome in the West is a sense of parental rejection. This is when one or both of our parents were more interested in pursuing their own individual needs than in being a mom or dad. This kind of rejection could be through abuse, divorce or neglect. We feel there's something wrong with us at our core, and if we don't receive healing through our relationship with the Father, we will spend the rest of our lives trying in various ways to get the affirmation we were denied. Some become hyper-competitive, feeling the endless need to prove themselves, chronically unable to rejoice in the success of others. Some medicate emptiness through a series of addictive and compulsive behaviors. For the sake of our kids and our relationship with God, let's get help. We must initiate a healing process. This will make us much better parents. The Gospel, through the power of the Holy Spirit, can heal us and renew our minds—make us new.

Digging Deeper

- Ransomed Heart - http://www.ransomedheart.com/

If you are reading the physical copy of this book you can find the links to the digging deeper resources at familyteams.com/FR.

TOOL #5 – THE TRAINING OF THE FAMILY

Joining the Team

"But I have calmed and quieted my soul, like a weaned child with its mother; like a weaned child is my soul within me." - Psalm 131:2

The moment a baby enters the world, she senses something is terribly wrong. She has no idea why these problems exist, but her natural reaction is to demand the problems get fixed and fast. "Give me warmth," "Give me milk," "Change my diaper," "Hold me," and the parents scurry around trying to discover the meaning of each cry in order to meet her every demand as best they can.

Moms and dads should fully enter into this phase, comforting their newborn and allowing their hearts to bond deeply with this precious new life. At the same time, one of the most important jobs the parents also have as their baby comes home and settles into her new world is integrating her into the family as a whole.

Since God has designed a family to function like a team, one of the first lessons babies must discover is that the world will not, cannot, does not and should not revolve around her desires alone. This is the first training exercise the parents engage in with their new family member. Over the first eighteen months, either the baby will be trained by her parents and siblings to take her place as a part of the team or she will train her parents and siblings to join the team that exists only to serve her.

This is often when we discover whether we believe the western philosophy of family or the biblical philosophy. Western parents cannot think of a good reason not to meet a baby's every desire. After all, they see themselves as individuals in pursuit of meeting their every desire and if they chose to have a child, then giving them whatever they want is what they've signed up for. No wonder parents with this philosophy have so few children. This kind of parenting is unsustainable and damaging for building a family team. God has already given the family a mission, and it is not to pamper children. Children exist to contribute to the family mission, not to subvert—and certainly not to redefine—that mission.

Each of our five babies has gone through a predictable transition at around 12-15 months. This often seems to happen shortly after a series of contests of will. They want something, they're old enough to know they want it, and that we can give it to them, and still, for reasons mysterious to them, we say no. They cry and try every tactic known to man to get us to change our minds. But through loving, consistent reinforcement of our leadership they eventually reach a state of complete acceptance. They discover, seemingly for the first time, that someone can cross their sovereign will and nothing they can do can alter the fact that we love them and at the same time we will not give in to them. Some children will make a trial of this in a variety of situations making sure it was just not a one--time occurrence.

Once they accept this new reality, that there is a will leading this family and it is not theirs, a deep new kind of calmness comes over the child, as if they had a great epiphany. They are not in charge. They are not the center. They are part of something bigger than themselves. They are a part of a team. Wise, consistent leadership is guiding the family. Sometimes they get what they want and sometimes they don't, but they don't decide when. On the surface this is not what children want, but it is what they desperately need and it creates in the child a true sense of security and the capacity for real joy. This is their first step into the family team and is also when much more training can begin. This is the moment, as their angry tears evaporate from their adorable little cheeks, where the family can say to the child, "Welcome to the team."

Digging Deeper

- [Online Course] The Skill of Fatherhood

If you are reading the physical copy of this book you can find the links to the digging deeper resources at familyteams.com/FR.

Teammate Training

"Train up a child in the way he should go; even when he is old he will not depart from it." - Proverbs 22:6

Once a child realizes they are being led by something outside their own immediate desires, they must be trained. You have successfully shown them what should not guide them; now you must show them what should. A lack of clear training at this point often results in children returning to a pattern of gratifying their immediate impulses as the guiding principle in their behavior.

Imagine if, after signing up for a team sport that you didn't even know how to play, you arrived with your teammates and the coach just sat around and occasionally barked out only what not to do. This is the state of most households. Modern families believe you should pamper up a child while conservative Christian families believe you should discipline up a child but the Bible tells us to train up a child. Training does not happen on accident. It's an intentional process. If we've embraced the biblical blueprint of the family becoming a team on a mission, then we must train our children.

One of the most challenging elements of training kids is to be aware and sensitive to the many transitions that take place throughout childhood. Each (often overlapping) stage offers new training challenges and opportunities, and there are many ways to break them down. Below is a very high-level description of training across the stages of a child's development.

For the first five years, parents are mostly training children simply to obey. This is often referred to as "The Cop Stage." This is not the end of training, but it's deep in the foundation and so must be done first. Children have learned obedience when they immediately and consistently obey their parent the first time the parent gives a command in a normal voice.

From ages five through seven, children learn to enjoy being a contributing member of the family. This is often referred to as "The Coach Stage." They are given tasks in which they can succeed and they make the family more functional, more efficient and more enjoyable through their initiative as a fully engaged part of the family team.

From ages eight through eleven, a child in a secure environment will be absorbed in a concrete kind of creativity and curiosity. This continues the phase of coaching while expanding the number of subjects.This is where children can learn how to learn. They are a huge sponge, can memorize vast amounts of information, ask great questions, and express what they're learning in creative ways. Parents during this stage can train their children both to go deep into a subject or skill and experience the fruits of determined perseverance as well as to go broad and explore a variety of different skills and experiences. This is when children often discover their talents. If the child shows great interest and aptitude toward something at which you are not skilled, then you should help find others in the wider community who can train your child in that area. During this season a child discovers and becomes increasingly proficient in unique areas that, when fully developed, will contribute greatly to their family team. Ages twelve through fifteen are the years when you bring your children into maturity. This is when a child learns personal responsibility and accountability. This is often referred to as "The Counselor Stage." Much of a family's training during this phase is focused on developing spiritual maturity. This must involve the child's individual pursuit of God so the child does not confuse her relationship with God with yours. This is another area where trusted members of a spiritual community can greatly help the family.

From around fifteen or sixteen, the basic foundational training should be nearing its completion; the child should be treated like a young man or woman and you should begin to take on more of a guiding role. This is often referred to as "The Consultant Stage." No matter your children's age, you should maintain a culture in the home that the mature child is required to respect, but you should also be careful not to overly control or constantly command your kids in this stage. They are accountable before God and so they need enough rope to feel the natural consequences of their behavior while still under your daily care and guidance.

Assist your children by developing a custom, balanced, training process for each season to further develop their talents, then help them discover avenues of integrating their new skills into the family in a way that blesses the whole family team.

Whole Team Training

"Fathers, do not exasperate your children; instead, bring them up in the training and instruction of the Lord." - **Ephesians 6:4**

When coaching a team, it's critical both to work with players individually, to prepare them to excel in their unique positions, and to train the team together to work as a whole. Teams that exude the kind of team spirit that makes them achieve far more together than they would separately have clear goals, a unified identity, strong leadership and a coordinated plan of attack.

By the nature of their basic design, families tend to have a strong, united identity. In this natural state families live in the same house, eat the same meals, work on the same projects, suffer the same misfortunes, have the same friends and extended family relations and protect the weaker members. It takes an alien, unnatural culture to create a family that eats separately, has separate friends, separate interests and identifies more strongly with a peer-based subculture than their own family. Most of what families must do to bring back a strong family identity involves resisting the forces that want to pull the family into its individual parts. In our family that means we don't worship separately, we worship together; we don't play sports separately but together; we don't learn separately but together; we eat most of our meals together; we make money together; we go on adventures together because we are one unit and we opt out of many opportunities that force us to spend too much time embodying our individual identities.

Once you begin to function more like a family rather than a network of individuals, it's important to find elements that will develop the fabric of your family team. Tendons join together our bones and muscles—many modern families have weak or non-existent tendons. When people think about your family as a whole, what comes to their minds? The more of these things you do, the more clear identifying markers you have, the stronger your internal identity becomes. What makes you the Parkers, the Carnegies, the Jeffersons? Building up that external identity is how you build up your internal identity. What ministries does your family do? What traditions? What missions? What adventures? What hobbies? What games? What kinds of businesses do you build? What kinds of art do you make? What languages do you speak? What holidays do you celebrate?

The second part to total team training is the training of the family leaders. If leading a strong family team was not modelled to the father or mother or both, then the family leaders must invest heavily in their own training. This can feel like we've been made the head coach of an important football team though we've never even played football let alone been trained to coach it. Give yourself a lot of grace. This is a multigenerational endeavor. You can make tremendous progress for your family in one generation but it will go much better if you can get some training. Become a keen observer of great mothers and fathers, and when you find them, intentionally get close to them and ask lots of questions. Integrate your life with them. Move into their home for a weekend, a week or a whole season. Continually refine and develop your understanding of fatherhood and motherhood. This is one big reason we have the body of Christ, our extended spiritual family.

For any team to really come together, they must train together. This should be done regularly, in a controlled environment appropriate to the age and maturity of the family, and in a way that brings out the unique strengths of your family's parts.

Our family spends four weeks per year on an RV adventure. This is mostly because we've had a baby in our family for more than 10 years so we needed an environment convenient enough to care for a baby but diverse enough to challenge the older kids. During these excursions, my primary focus is training the family together. How do they handle the repetitive chores, getting on each other's nerves during travel times, and new and sometimes dangerous environments. When I see a failing in how the kids relate I need to remember, this isn't game time, it's practice. So I take the kids aside, walk them through the correct way to handle that situation and insist that they try again. We actually practice being a team. Each night we debrief and discuss what each member of our family team has learned. Our family's cohesion as a team in protecting each other's unique weaknesses and releasing each other strengths and overall love and compassion for each other has now reached the point we can play bigger and bigger "games."

We spent two and half months in Jerusalem this year where we walked everywhere, often a foot away from busy streets with mopeds on the sidewalk, and our kids snapped into action, caring for each other and working as a unit. This didn't happen by accident or through strict discipline but years of intentional, repeated training. Some of the family teams in our extended community take weekend hiking and camping trips every month. Imagine how much great family training Jewish families experienced as they took pilgrimages to Jerusalem three times per year. Western families need times like this if they are going to transition into finely tuned family teams.

TOOLS FOR FAMILY TRAINING

Melting the Hearts of your Kids with the Gospel

"'My son,' the father said, 'you are always with me, and everything I have is yours. But we had to celebrate and be glad, because this brother of yours was dead and is alive again; he

was lost and is found.'" - **Luke 15:31-32**

The most critical family training is what I think of simply as gospel training. Every family has a culture. Most modern families exude a culture of individualism, but some families build their culture on things like honor, training kids to be proud of their family and telling them "we are too good to act like this or that". We want our family to have a strong culture but not one built on pride. We want our family to have a gospel culture. The Gospel has the power to give a family a powerful self-image, one that is strong but not proud and humble but not timid. Only the story of the Gospel can shape a family culture in a way that will help your kids fall in love with Christ while each one is transformed by His grace.

This is because the Gospel story gives us an identity as freed slaves. We have a humble and downright humiliating past. Our ancient family wilfully chose to rebel against the rightful ruler of the world and became slaves to sin. Every Sabbath we have our kids tell the story of our enslavement through a question and answer time. I bring out a box and ask the kids what this represents and they say, "That we were locked away in slavery." Surprised, I then say, "Really! When were we slaves? How did that happen? So was it our fault? Are we still slaves today? How were we freed?" We began this tradition because Deuteronomy 5:15 says, "Remember that you were once slaves in Egypt, but the Lord your God brought you out with his strong hand and powerful arm. That is why the Lord your God has commanded you to rest on the Sabbath day." God was concerned that future descendants of the Israelites would lose their identity as freed slaves and become proud and forget the Lord once they were safe in the Promised Land. And if you are raising your children in a Christian environment, then your children are at great risk of losing this identity as well. Christian kids tend to take their salvation for granted. They often say a prayer for salvation when they're very young and believe they are basically a good kid, deserving to be saved. Like the older brother in the Prodigal Son story, they look down their noses and judge those who struggle with more obvious forms of sin. Without Gospel training you will, by default, raise a bunch of Pharisees—with maybe a black sheep or two—who feel they can't measure up.

As you tell the story of our freedom from slavery week after week and celebrate our salvation in Christ, you will discover if it's sinking in by seeing who your kids relate to when they are in a mixed environment. Someone who truly sees their past as a criminal and slave will naturally identify with those who are marginalized. They will look at those kids who are picked on, poor, or even downright mean and say in their heart, "That was me until Christ rescued me." They will have compassion and patience because of their shared identity with these troubled kids. A judgemental spirit—"I hope they get what they deserve" or "They are bad and I am good"—is clear evidence that the opposite of a gospel culture is emerging in your home.

The strongest tool we use to help form a Gospel culture for our kids is "Gospel Week" where, every day from Palm Sunday through Resurrection Sunday we vividly portray what it took to rescue us (Galatians 3:1). What melts kids' hearts and causes them to truly fall in love with Jesus is a deep understanding and appreciating of what salvation really costs.

But like everything else in parenting, you can only pass on what you yourself deeply believe. That is why Paul doesn't say you minister in proportion to your skill but you minister in proportion to your faith (Romans 12:6). I realized that my faith in the Gospel was too weak and I set aside a whole year and almost exclusively studied the Gospel until my heart broke over and over with what Christ did for me. Then, out of my brokenness, I tried to find ways to express my heart to my family. This was when I really saw my kids' hearts start to change.

Digging Deeper

- [Audio] <u>Equipping Households to Celebrate the Spring Holidays</u> - In this mp3 I describe some elements of how we designed Gospel Week. I'm working on a much better 2.0 version of Gospel Week I'll teach on in 2012 and post here.
- [Audio] <u>Tim Keller's Gospel Sermons</u> - My year of studying the Gospel began by listening to Tim Keller's Gospel sermons many of which you can get for free on this site.
- [Book] <u>The Jesus Storybook Bible</u> - Based on Tim Keller's teaching this book for children tells the story of the Gospel through many various stories throughout the Bible.

If you are reading the physical copy of this book you can find the links to the digging deeper resources at <u>familyteams.com/FR</u>.

Applying the Gospel to the Problems of the Heart

"Tell your children of it, and let your children tell their children, and their children to another generation". - Joel 1:3

Tim Keller once explained, "Every problem we have is because we are forgetting to apply some aspect of the Gospel to our hearts." If you agree with this statement, as I do, then the implications for parenting are enormous.

Having five kids, we've dealt with a large range of issues from religious perfectionism to outright rebellion and found the Gospel is the unique antidote to helping kids work through the diseases of sin that infect their hearts. This goes a step beyond training our kids in the Gospel in general and working with them to discover how the Gospel applies to their specific set of issues.

For example, if one of our kids is struggling with perfectionism and beats herself down whenever she makes a mistake or strives to get her approval from her performance, then the Gospel says something unique to her. She believes if she is just good enough then she will be justified; she's forgetting she is already justified—that no matter how amazing her performance, the last word has already been spoken about her value at the cross. She needs to boast in the cross, to look at Jesus in the face dying in her place and say to her heart, "Look how much He loves me." This will forever transform her identity. Once her heart begins to trust in Christ's work on the cross for her justification, she will be forever free of the ruthless taskmaster of perfectionism to provide her justification. She will be filled with an unmovable joy because her value is set forever. She will believe she is of tremendous value because of what it cost to save her and, at the same time, she will become increasingly humble because her sin caused Jesus to pay that price.

Other children struggle with a rebellious spirit. They don't want to submit to Jesus as Lord and believe their life would be better if they were running it themselves. They see Christianity as the opposite of freedom. Kids who run from God in this way either don't know or don't fully identify with the backstory of the Gospel—that we already are rebels, and look at what it cost us and what it cost God to bring us back. Families that enjoy celebrating the whole Gospel story from slavery back into the Kingdom form children that believe the story of the Gospel and see rebellion as a return to a terrible past way of life and an insult to the Savior who gave up so much to bring them home.

Even when the antidote of the Gospel story is pulsing through the veins of your children, the Gospel will still often need to be rehearsed to confront various idols that try to take root in their lives. When we see our kids fall in love with video games, popularity, sports or themselves, we often spend all of our energy attacking the idols themselves but the Gospel presents a different approach. The only way to break the hold of a beautiful object on the soul is to show it an object more beautiful (to paraphrase Thomas Chalmers's famous sermon "The Expulsive Power of a New Affection"). It's not enough just to say no—we need to give our kids something greater to which they can say yes. The greatest antidote for sin is not always more self-control but greater spiritual passion. The Gospel gives kids this passion for Christ. When they see what it cost Him and how glorious His love truly is, spiritual passion will begin to violently shove out the idols in their lives.

If you would like to have a home where the enemy is given no access to your children's hearts, where his lies are repulsive to them, then you must train your children in the wonder and beauty of the Gospel and show how it infiltrates every part of their lives.

Childhood Education

"And these words that I command you today shall be on your heart. You shall teach them diligently to your children, and shall talk of them when you sit in your house, and when you walk by the way, and when you lie down, and when you rise."
Deuteronomy 6:6-7

Western culture sees education as the primary focus for kids ages 5-18. It seems so obvious to us we never question this belief. We can't even imagine what we would do with kids if we didn't center their lives around their individual education. This has always made complete sense to me but I wanted to make sure what I did with my children was based on the firm foundation of Scripture so I asked a dangerous question: "If all I had to go on was the Bible, what would I think was the primary activity for children?" I searched Scripture for any place where God seemed to outline what kids were to do with their time and the clearest passage I could find was the one above from Deuteronomy 6. It affirmed that we are to teach our children so, yes education is important, but what we educate kids about, who educates our kids, how we educate kids and even where we educate kids was also spelled out in surprising detail. God commands parents to teach their children's hearts the things God commands. He tells us to do this by talking constantly to our kids and he expects this will happen around the normal activities of daily life.

None of this seems to suggest educating in other areas, in other ways, or at other places is prohibited. Families have a lot of freedom in trying to find ways to shape their children's education, but one important thing to consider is how to create a Deuteronomy 6 culture in your family as a major part of their educational experience. How can this be done practically?

First, never stop finding creative ways to integrate your kids into more elements of your normal daily life. The underlying assumption of Deuteronomy 6 is that your kids are with you a lot. Anytime I go anywhere, my base assumption is I should take one of my kids with me. That could be a walk to the convenience store or on an international business trip. This is not always possible but I work really hard to be with my kids as much as I possibly can. I'm highly introverted so this can be costly in terms of my energy but it's really worth it and is a critical part of their education. Our culture has developed this strange dichotomy between quality time and quantity time—maybe to make us feel better about the decreasing amount of time we spend with our kids—but there's no substitute for quantity time. The most basic secret to increasing quality time is to increase quantity time.

One experiment I've been trying for over a decade is allowing well-behaved kids to have unlimited access to their parents during the work day. At my office you'll see kids everywhere with their parents. In between meetings, parents are directing their kids' activities, and their kids can walk around the office and meet their parents' colleagues, learn about what we do and feel at home interacting with one another. This was a direct result of trying to apply Deuteronomy 6.

Once you have much more quantity time with your kids, your job is simply to talk to them all the time. Just say out loud what you're thinking and why you're doing what you're doing, especially in areas where it applies to the intersection between life and faith.

It's common for me to take each of my five kids on a day with Dad every week. I noticed in the car that I was getting lost in my own thoughts and not talking with my kids. Even when I became focused on the child, I couldn't always come up with interesting topics to discuss on the fly. So I bought a box of questions called the "Ungame," and it's been a huge game-changer. Anytime I'm in the car with one of my kids, I have them pull a card out of the box, read the question and answer it and bam, we're immediately into a deep conversation.

Every family has very different constraints and opportunities when trying to create an educational culture that reflects Deuteronomy 6. Just start with one idea at a time by asking how can I have more frequent conversations with my kids throughout the week.

TOOL #6 – THE RESOURCES OF THE FAMILY

Ending Work-based Identities

***"And God blessed them. And God said to them, "Be fruitful and multiply and fill the earth and subdue it..."* -Genesis 1:28**

"What do you want to be when you grow up?" This question, along with the constant message, "You can be anything you want to be," attempts to train kids from a very young age that their work will define their identity and that this decision is entirely up to them. But are these messages biblical? These kinds of questions and statements betray the search for identity and significance our culture engages in apart from God. Author David Dunlap wrote that western people, "[W]orship their work, work at their play, and play at their worship".

Work is important beyond simply providing for our basic needs. Work can be the way we minister to the world and fulfill our creation mandate to be fruitful, to rule and to subdue the Earth. When we work well, we bring order to chaos. But it's also important to note that in Genesis 1-2, when God saw all the work that needed to be done, he didn't create a single gardener—he created a whole family. The mandate to bring order is primarily a family mandate and not simply given to us as individuals.

Work began in the garden of Eden, before the Fall. Adam and Eve and their future children were to tend the garden and expand it. Their work was blessed. Providing for themselves was relatively easy and they were able to rest one day a week and in the evenings as they walked with God in the cool of the day. But after the Fall, work was cursed. It became hard. It became toil. We had to work longer, harder, smarter and do things we hated and were bad at simply to have enough to eat. Now when a company hires a worker who is a part of a family, they often try to downplay or completely ignore their family identity. When we walk through the doors of your workplace, we are a piece of that company and so we're often encouraged to leave our family identities at home. While we can't stop our employers or staff from thinking this way, it's critical we don't take on this mindset ourselves.

Every day when I work, I think of myself primarily as an agent of my family. My family needs financial resources today so they sent me out to get some and bring them back. Whether I find deep satisfaction from the work itself is less important than whether what I've accomplish satisfies the needs of my family. This attachment to family and detachment from particular kinds of work is essential if fathers and mothers are to make wise choices about how they provide. I spent years making money in e-commerce, then in internet marketing, and now in video production. While I enjoy all of these industries, my passion for these lines of work has never been able to compete with my passion for my family or my identity as a father.

Work allows us to minister to a broken world, grow as individuals, and provide for our families. Work in this family context is the coordinated effort to bring enough resources into the family to provide for basic needs, long-term security, financial independence and multigenerational cohesion. The most effective expression of this activity happens when a father and mother help the family acquire multigenerational assets.

Stewarding Assets vs. Lifelong Employment

"Do your planning and prepare your fields before building your house." -**Proverbs 24:27**

There are two primary ways you can provide income for your family. The first is by going out and trading your time for money. This is also called getting a job. While this is often an effective and honorable way of providing for one's family, this is a highly unusual way of making money throughout the Bible. All the great fathers in the Bible provided for their families through another method we're going to refer to simply as stewarding assets. They would own land, livestock or trade skills, and the family would work together to expand those resources to provide larger and more secure streams of revenue for their present and future needs.

As I and many of my friends have tried both of these methods for providing for our families we've noticed that stewarding assets tends to have many advantages over regular employment when attempting to develop a family team. Here are some of the advantages -

- Daily Time - Stewards get to design a family-friendly rhythm while employees normally have to work within a business-friendly rhythm.
- Annual Time - Stewards can design an annual rhythm where the needs and opportunities of the family instead of the cycle of the business can influence their time off.
- Flex Time - Stewards can reduce the hours they work during times where provision is abundant and increase the amount of time they invest when income contracts; employees are often forced to

commit to a fixed amount of time every week.

- Family Involvement - Stewards can devise ways of including their family in stewarding and expanding their assets, allowing the family to work as a team; employees are often restricted to a once-per-year take-your-child-to-work day.
- Multigenerational Blessings - Stewards can pass on assets to their children and grandchildren.
- Living Location - Stewarding assets often brings adult children and extended family together to a location where they can work together; employees are often moved to the location that best suits their employer.
- Security - Owning and stewarding multiple assets can lead to more security as the asset matures because you own the income source; an employee can lose their job at any time and their job may become obsolete or outsourced over time.
- Family Needs - Stewards can flex when a child needs lots of special attention or when mom is sick or when dad needs to get more involved in schooling the kids.
- Blessing - Owning assets allows God to pour abundant blessing into things you own if He wants to entrust you with more resources; employment doesn't create as natural a way to receive abundant blessing.
- Generosity - When assets provide surges of revenue instead of the fixed revenue provided by employment, this can allow for surges of generosity which transforms the giver in unique ways.
- Training - Stewarding assets provides constant holistic training where you cannot blame your boss but only yourself for mistakes.
- Ethics - Stewarding assets forces the family to

make and stand by difficult ethical decisions like how to treat workers, what to charge, how to treat the environment and many others.

Employment can be a great short-term way of gaining the money to buy assets (as long as you live way below your means) or for getting through tough seasons, but I'd challenge any family who thinks employment is a better long-term or permanent strategy for solving the problem of family provision. Most of us have just assumed it was our only option. Our society is obsessed with employment.

This is another area where Christians have been more shaped by popular western culture than the Bible. So let's look at how the Bible models asset-building as the normal means of family provision.

Digging Deeper

- [Book] Rich Dad Poor Dad (What the Rich Teach Their Kids About Money--That the Poor and the Middle Class Do Not!)- If you struggle with what I've written PLEASE read this book.
- [Book] Self-Made in America - While I don't believe anyone is truly self-made this collection of stories of immigrants who came with nothing to America, lived in poverty and became owners of valuable assets was quite instructive and inspirational

If you are reading the physical copy of this book you can find the links to the digging deeper resources at familyteams.com/FR.

Stewardship in the Bible

"The inheritance of the people of Israel shall not be transferred

from one tribe to another, for every one of the people of Israel shall hold on to the inheritance of the tribe of his fathers." - **Numbers 36:7**

The primary place I've discovered instruction and inspiration for stewarding assets is the Bible. Beginning with the patriarchs Abraham, Isaac and Jacob, we're given a great introduction for how stewardship works, how it provides blessing for our families, and how it is intricately connected to our relationship with God.

God tells Abram he will bless his multigenerational family and Abram's response was to take his assets and go on a faith journey toward a land God would show him (Genesis 12). Western people don't fully appreciate how wealthy Abraham really was and how his wealth continued to increase under God's blessing. We learn in Genesis 13 that "Abram had become very wealthy in livestock and in silver and gold" and between Abraham and Lot "the land could not support them while they stayed together, for their possessions were so great that they were not able to stay together." We further learn in Genesis 14 that, after Lot was captured, Abram "called out the 318 trained men born in his household." Which means if you add women, children and older or untrained men Abraham's household must have had over 1000 servants. In other words there were many servants (employees) during Abraham's time but God chose to tell His story through a family of asset-owners.

This theme continues with Isaac, where the longest chapter about his leadership of the family is Genesis 26, in which Isaac negotiates with a regional king to establish his family's water rights. Again, the narrative paints the picture of a father who expands family assets. Then when Jacob begins in poverty after fleeing from Esau, he works for Laban until he is married then he says, "You know how I have worked for you and how your livestock has fared under my care. The little you had before I came has increased greatly, and the LORD has blessed you wherever I have been. But now, when may I do something for my own household?" (Genesis 30:29-30) In other words, Jacob's perspective was that getting only a living wage from Laban as an employee was only helping Laban's household, not Jacob's. Jacob tells Laban he only wants to be paid in assets (livestock) and he trusted the Lord to bless his family by increasing those assets. The abundance that resulted is a major theme of the rest of Jacob's narrative.

"Well that's fine for a minority of people," someone may say, "but you can't have an entire culture of asset-owners." However, when God set out to design an economy for Israel, he did exactly that. God designed it in a way that every family could be like the patriarchs and make its living through stewarding assets. After conquering the Promised Land, each family was given land rights, water rights, and very specific boundaries with villages in the center of their land where they could trade. We don't see any example of someone having a career as a permanent replacement to being an asset-owner. Many have tried to suggest that the Levites were a professional class who passed on a job instead of land but they apparently have never read Joshua 21 where the Levites were given towns and pasture lands, including Aaron's family. Consider just the sheer number of Holy Spirit-inspired verses in Scripture dedicated to making clear this asset allotment (like Joshua 13-21). Having specific skills, whether it be as a craftsman, warrior or priest, did not mean you were on a different path as a career man while others were asset-builders. Your specialization was just another asset in the form of a small business you would steward to increase or secure your other assets.

Maintaining this asset stewardship culture was so important to God that He invented an elaborate economic system that dealt with every possible threat to its long-term viability. A family who doesn't produce a male heir could pass on the land to a female (Numbers 36). A wife whose husband died before producing an heir could have a child with the next of kin and all the land rights of the family would pass to that child (Deuteronomy 25). A family that foolishly goes into debt would have their debt forgiven every seven years (Deuteronomy 15:1-11). A family who loses their land in one generation would get it all back in the next generation during the year of Jubilee (Leviticus 25). A family who has to become employees of another family would need to be set free every seven years (Deuteronomy 15:12-18). And an Israelite who sells their ancestral land or their lives to a foreigner would be redeemed by the next of kin during the year of Jubilee and buy the land or family members back from the foreigner and restore it to the original family (Leviticus 25). Imagine what this meant. Every generation would would start out as asset-stewards with the goal of working their own land. In fact when Micah talks about what life will be like in God's future Kingdom, he describes it using the Hebrew phrase for family financial independence: "Everyone will sit under their own vine and under their own fig tree" (Micah 4:4). Today our longest-term goal tends to be to help make our children great stewards of the assets of others families.

The only real weakness in this system of asset ownership is that, in most cultures, after a few generations, all the assets end up in the hands of the few families who are committed to multigenerational asset ownership. In other words, it works too well. In the face of a strong family committed to working together to acquiring and expanding assets over multiple generations, no other economic endeavors can compete in the long-term. Eventually 1-2% of the families will own 80% of any country's resources. That's because what creates abundance or poverty in a free society is primarily a mindset. It's simply having a long-term vision for asset ownership, stewardship and expansion. So what if we trained every family to steward assets? What if we helped all families adopt a multigenerational mindset toward stewarding resources?

Some who read these lessons from the Old Testament believe the New Testament somehow replaced these ideas. So let's turn now and consider how the New Testament talks about families and finances.

Digging Deeper

- [Book] Thou Shall Prosper - Rabbi Daniel Lapin dives deep into the Old Testament and Jewish culture to help readers understand a uniquely Jewish way of viewing money and business.

If you are reading the physical copy of this book you can find the links to the digging deeper resources at familyteams.com/FR.

Family Financial Independence

"Make it your goal to live a quiet life, minding your own business and working with your hands, just as we instructed you before. Then people who are not Christians will respect the way you live, and you will not need to depend on others." - **1 Thessalonians 4:11-12**

Most Christians do not seem to know that the Bible commands believing families to make it their goal to achieve financial independence (1 Thessalonians 4:11-12). Paul lays it out: this process begins with having a clear objective, working hard with your own resources until you are no longer dependent on others.

Paul stewarded a trade skill, making tents in various cities he traveled through as he pointed out to the Ephesians elders reminding them: "You know that these hands of mine have worked to supply my own needs (Acts 20:34)." Paul was a single man and so his life was extremely minimalistic compared to a man needing to provide for a large household. Which brings up the one major area where the New Testament speaks while the Old Testament is silent: the honorable, simple, single life.

Jesus demonstrated what it's like to live a simple, single life, and encouraged others to consider this new lifestyle (Matthew 19:12) as does the Apostle Paul (1 Corinthians 7). Those who are content to be single should seek to give themselves fully to the Lord (1 Corinthians 7:32), which is a radically different path than a family seeking financial independence.

We have an epidemic in today's church of married people living like singles. They follow the lifestyle example of Jesus or Paul instead of Abraham and they focus countless hours on ministry while neglecting their responsibilities as husbands and fathers. If you choose to be single, then feel free follow the lifestyle example of Christ which may include: living on the side of the road (Luke 9:58), catching fish to find money to pay your taxes (Matthew 17:27) and during intense seasons of mission, receiving donations and financial support from friends and family for your very few physical needs (Luke 8:3). But if you start a family, then you are on an entirely different path. For your family's sake, make it your goal to become financially self-sufficient. When it comes to building family resources, the Old and New Testament speak with one voice.

When it comes to money, there's no question the New Testament warns against worry (Matthew 6:25), greed (Colossians 3:5) or the desire to become wealthy (1 Timothy 6:9). But these warnings should not be seen as contradicting the model of stewarding assets given to families in the Old Testament or the connected command to work toward financial independence in the New Testament. Christian families must question the west's debt-ridden, career-obsessed culture and understand the Bible has a superior understanding of economics and finances that leads to greater security, generosity and freedom.

Digging Deeper

- [Slide Share] <u>The New Testament Single Life</u> - In this presentation I walk through the 3 lifestyles described for singles in the New Testament and a possible proposals for how families and singles can work together on our mission to make disciples.

If you are reading the physical copy of this book you can find the links to the digging deeper resources at <u>familyteams.com/FR</u>.

TOOLS FOR BUILDING RESOURCES FOR YOUR FAMILY TEAM

Stages of Gaining Financial Freedom

"Wealth gained hastily will dwindle, but whoever gathers little by little will increase it." **-Proverbs 13:11**

If the idea of asset management as a solution for family provision is new to you and you're interested in moving this direction, then you're probably wondering how to get started. As we've watched many families make this transition, we've noticed a lot of common stages they seem to go through. In order to make this really practical, I'll describe these stages and what's normally involved in each.

The first phase involves financial reeducation. Because most issues regarding finances and resources really stem from a lack of understanding in these important areas, families must go through a complete relearning process. Many of the books I've recommended above are read, studied and discussed. Having a mentor or someone who is currently much farther along on the road you're wanting to go down is extremely valuable.

Once families begin to really understand what money, debt, assets, and resources are really all about, they will typically work to do two things in parallel: increase income and decrease expenses. If they have debt, they will realize how dangerous, foolish and unbiblical (Romans 13:8) most debts are and craft an aggressive debt payoff plan. They will also look to leverage any immediate assets they have to create additional income streams.

"But how do I create income streams large enough to achieve financial freedom?" everyone wants to know. Let's be clear on the long-term goal first. The kinds of assets that create the highest level of freedom are stable, capital-intensive assets like rental properties or lots of stock in a diverse set of stable companies. As the saying goes, "You concentrate money to create wealth and you diversify to keep it."

In a wealthy country like the United States, the average person dedicated to this task could achieve it through employment in about 30 years. This can be done simply by working the highest-paying job you can find and investing 10-20% of your income every year in stable investments. Just to put this in perspective, people in most countries around the world would love to have the opportunity you have; the vast majority of them couldn't hope to achieve that goal in ten lifetimes. That's why so many are risking everything to move to wealthier, more stable countries.

But here's the real problem—westerners almost universally refuse to live a lifestyle several levels below those who make their same income level. If their friends are living in nice houses, they won't be content in a small apartment or driving old cars. If we're honest, it isn't because we can't build assets—we're just unwilling to pay the price. The first step of this price is to shield yourself from the endless advertising designed to make you discontented. Try and strip away any sources of entertainment you consume that involve advertising.

Are there ways families can shorten the 30-year process of gaining financial independence? Yes, but they involve more risk. The fastest way a family with very little capital can work to shorten the time it takes to accumulate income -producing assets is by getting equity in the early stages of a new business. One of the most common myths we need to dispel is the feeling many have that they have to be an entrepreneur to become a steward of assets. Any and every family can steward income-producing assets of some type. But being an entrepreneur, when you're starting with nothing, is usually the fastest way to reach the goal.

In our community there are three ways families make additional streams of income through new businesses. The first is being an entrepreneur who starts new businesses. The second is being a great partner to an entrepreneur who is starting a new business. And the third is taking over a growing business an entrepreneur has started, but no longer has the energy or expertise to continue developing. In each case, what the family asked for was equity (a percentage of ownership in the business) and not just income. Remember the goal is not to land a better job but to help your family achieve financial independence. In our community, the average number of years to financial independence through business ownership is about 10 years. Whenever possible, we need to network with other families and help one another. Particularly if you've found success, immediately find ways to help other families gain the financial position you've achieved.

Digging Deeper

- [Course] <u>Financial Peace University</u> - For families drowning in debt your first step should be to learn from Dave Ramsey.
- [Website] <u>Getting Rich Slowly</u> - An entire site dedicated to the slow, careful acquisition of income producing assets.
- [Website] <u>Springwise</u> - A site that spots amazing innovative ideas around the world which can be great inspiration for finding a business model to bring to your area.
- [Post] <u>Transitioning Pastors from Paid Positions to Released Callings (Part 1), (Part 2), (Part 3), (Part 4).</u>

If you are reading the physical copy of this book you can find the links to the digging deeper resources at <u>familyteams.com/FR</u>.

Building Assets in Community

"One who has unreliable friends soon comes to ruin, but there is a friend who sticks closer than a brother." **-Proverbs 18:24**

Many people believe family or friendships and business just don't mix. If that's because they've seen or experienced partnerships with someone with a different view of money and business, completely different goals, or those without faith in the power of the Gospel to heal and found relationships, then they're probably right. Relationships and money can be sticky business indeed. It takes great love for each other, persistent humility and the decision to submit to Scripture to define family, money and business. But if these things are in place, if both parties have the same Kingdom mindset toward family, money and the Gospel, then business partnerships can unleash a diverse force so powerful that the chance of success is greatly increased.

The power of a solid partnership is undeniable. You get to leverage all the skills of one or more families from day one. When everyone is working for ownership and none of the families are draining revenue out of the business early on, the more people with the right skills who can put time and energy into the company and wait for the long-term return, the better.

The problem with partnering is primarily relational. In the world, people are often self-focused, have nothing objective to appeal to when they disagree, and value their own comfort above the relationship. But faith in the Gospel can redeem broken relationships. That is why in the Kingdom, we have a tremendous business advantage. We can partner, and instead of business destroying our relationships, these partnerships can build our relationship, all the while giving us an amazing leg up in today's hyper-competitive marketplace.

I have been in business partnerships with many of my closest friends and almost every member of my family. It has not been easy. Relationally, there have been great years and hard years, but my overall experience has been that as long as love, humility and the Gospel rule the hearts of each one of us, we can overcome the relational challenges that inevitably arise in business.

Our family has started three different businesses and several nonprofit ventures in partnership with the Mowry family. Stephen Mowry has been a faithful friend to me through grueling seasons of business startup, exciting seasons of business success and challenging seasons of business decline. The love and loyalty our families have needed to show to each other have made our lives far more rich and our businesses much more successful.

Where this starts for most families is very slowly and carefully. Instead of coming up with a business idea and finding a family you barely know and trying to start a partnership, I recommend building stable, long-standing relationships with other families and agreeing to partner with a family after you've established a deep relational connection. You choose a business model together and step into the wild world of business, founding the company on the strength of your family relationship. You protect that relationship through transparency, humility and regular rhythms of communication. You work to bless each other and you show love, concern and complete solidarity with each other's family.

Digging Deeper

- [Book] The Partnership Charter - Do not start your partnership without reading a book like this and getting the necessary details of the partnership in writing. People think if you really trust each other a handshake is all that's needed. Far from demonstrating trust, this kind of presumption is more often disrespectful to the relationship. The best way to protect the long-term health of your business relationships is to have the hard conversations first, and David Gage does a great job in this book describing how to structure those conversations and the partnership agreement.

If you are reading the physical copy of this book you can find the links to the digging deeper resources at familyteams.com/FR.

The Generous Family

*"The generous will prosper; those who refresh others will themselves be refreshed." -***Proverbs 11:25**

One of the greatest and most consistent fruits of family-based stewardship of resources is the outpouring of abundant generosity. Living on a fixed income determined by someone else on a fixed work schedule dictated by someone else who works to direct your best energy toward their ends can leave us with a sense of powerlessness with little left over to give to others. Faced with the frustration this can often create, it becomes easier just to give ourselves over to our work identity. When we do, we tend to live a disintegrated life, always needing to guard against additional commitments since we often have to fight to give our family enough of what they need from whatever is left over, which can put a damper on a spirit of abundant generosity.

Contrast that with income streams that produce money in ways that aren't directly connected to how many hours you worked this week. This begins to disentangle the connection between our time and energy and our money.

We know that when the resources we're stewarding expand and multiply, we're being blessed by God. As things naturally grow and produce more resources, giving back in radical ways feels natural and even needed. Not to give generously wouldn't be merely stinginess, but a complete breakdown in integrity since these are God's resources, He's multiplying them, and we as stewards are responsible for discerning what things He wants us to bless in turn. "So neither the one who plants nor the one who waters is anything, but only God, who makes things grow." 1 Corinthians 3:7

Because this kind of lifestyle is so different from the typical mentality of most 9-to-5 western employees, families who choose to steward their resources must learn an alternate pattern for determining how they give of their time, money and energy.

How many hours per week should you work? How much vacation time should you spend? Can you spend weeks or months at a time creating art, ministering on a mission trip, educating your family? These questions are less relevant when working as an employee from paycheck to paycheck, but they constantly come up with someone who is stewarding resources. What do you do when you could work 20 hours per week and both meet all of your expenses and continue to grow and expand your resources? Should you just work 40 hours per week since that's what most employees do? Should you work 70 hours per week since you're the "owner" and you need to make sure everyone is doing their job? Many people who start businesses trade a fixed 40-hour-per-week job working for someone else for an 80-hour-per-week job working for the hardest and most unreasonable taskmaster, themselves. But who are you working for when you steward resources? Don't forget that you are God's steward and He wants the largest return for his Kingdom as you can give him from every area of your life. This means as God blesses our efforts, we must reevaluate where we allocate our time.

In our family, we created a trigger in our lives that helped us break out of the traditional work-week mold. We decided that the first month our income overcame our expenses, we would set a significant number of hours per week aside to do Kingdom ministry. We would use some of the excess money produced by our resources to hire a skilled business manager to free up the resource that had become more scarce than money—our time. Becoming generous with our time was where radical generosity began with our family within the first two years of our lifestyle of stewarding resources.

We also look for ways to be generous with our energy, of which there are different kinds. There's just plain task energy where you answer emails, work on concrete projects and run errands. There's relational energy where you spend time with people (and as introverts my wife and I both try and carefully allocate this limited resource). And there's creative energy where we write, develop new business models, prepare for talks and exert creativity in a variety of ways. For many years I gave virtually all of my creative energy to growing our assets. But today I try to give away this valuable resource to Kingdom projects, and having the freedom not to hand all of that resource over to an employer has allowed for this new kind of generosity.

Being generous with money is a bit more concrete but no less powerful than being generous with our time or energy. The great thing about being generous with money is that it doesn't have fixed limits like time or energy. Giving money is a powerful creative act that brings things into being that otherwise wouldn't exist. Freeing up other people's time or energy and growing resources for the Kingdom that pour out God's blessing around the world is the fruit of financial giving.

The more God blesses our resources, the more we've experienced the amazing blessing of giving. Jesus made it clear that the amount of a gift is not paramount when He pointed out the small gift of the widow at the temple; giving with that kind of abandon, when you're also responsible for providing for your family, makes more sense when you steward resources where God can then turn around and double your income in one month through a new client, finding a new tenant, having a new business idea or countless other ways resources can expand or multiply.

As I prayed one day, God gave me a picture of a large basin in which He wanted to pour His blessing. He showed me that I was largely responsible for making sure the basin was ready and wasn't full of cracks. He showed me areas of waste in the business we owned and made it clear that I needed to steward the basin better—but that He was going to fill it.

I believe God still wants every family to have a basin in which He can pour blessing. Stewarding that basin is great for our own discipleship and maturity, and releasing that blessing into His Kingdom is the amazing gift we get to receive as skillful and faithful stewards of His endless resources. This, after all, is what He's ultimately preparing us for. He wants his sons and daughters to grow up and be mature enough to know how to steward his Kingdom when we rise to reign with him forever and ever.

Digging Deeper

- [Book] The E-Myth Revisited - Every family growing assets through business ownership who wants to give time to the Kingdom must learn to work ON their business instead of IN their business.

If you are reading the physical copy of this book you can find the links to the digging deeper resources at familyteams.com/FR.

Passing on Resources to the Next Generation

"Good people leave an inheritance to their grandchildren, but the sinner's wealth passes to the godly." **-Proverbs 13:22**

Is it really a blessing to pass vast resources on to the next generation? Is it a smart thing to do spiritually? For thousands of years, those with a more classical model of family would have considered giving nothing to your children to be, at best, a failure of parenthood and at worst, a death sentence. But in a relatively safe society of economic abundance, many parents, especially Christian parents, feel passing down considerable financial resources to actually be a curse. How do we navigate this divide?

It was certainly normal and important for families in Israel to pass on family resources to the next generation ("Houses and wealth are inherited from parents..." Proverbs 19:14) but in western culture, doesn't giving your kids what amounts to a free ride destroy their motivation? If you simply hand kids money without condition, without vision, and without training, the answer certainly is yes. You create in kids a sense of entitlement where you implicitly communicate to your kids that the only vision for stewarding the family wealth is the expansion of their own comfort and the indulgence of their every flesh-driven desire. What a mess. This is not healthy for kids. Under these circumstances, it would be far better to give your kids nothing.

But there is another way. Once again, the answer lies in a deep understanding of the role of a steward. God wants to be able to entrust His stewards, His sons and daughters, with HIs abundant resources. But can we handle it? How can he know?

Jesus shows us exactly how our heavenly Father makes this determination, and it provides a perfect pattern for parents wanting to build a strong, lasting, influential multigenerational family. In Luke 19 (and in other Gospels) Jesus tells a story of a King entrusting money to three stewards. When the King returns for an accounting, he gives more resources to those who have multiplied his smaller initial investment. The King was testing these stewards. This is largely what life is like in the Kingdom today. We have the Kingdom in part, and what we do during this age will determine our role when the Kingdom comes in its fullness.

Families must set up similar tests for their children. Remember the resources you have are not yours and you don't owe them to your children. To simply give each child an equal share regardless of their fitness to steward God's resources is both bad stewardship on your part and evidence that you really believe the resources belong to you and your family to do with them whatever you please.

While you are still alive you must entrust more and more of your resources to the children in your family who are the most skilled and most faithful stewards. You must train your kids from an early age to understand that these resources do not exist for our family's comfort. We don't increase the luxury of our lifestyle when God blesses us, we increase the faithfulness of our stewardship.

So why not just leave any and all resources to an effective Christian ministry or non-profit organization that is set up to steward resources? If none of your children are fit to steward the King's resources, then this is a possible plan B, but those resources could do far more good in the hands of a faithful multigenerational, visionary family.

It's certainly important to give generously to organizations and ministries whose mission you believe in while keeping in mind that families have the potential to be better stewards *over the long term* than organizations. Families are holistic in that they can both continue to invest and expand the resources as well as continually manage the direction of the resources. Multigenerational family teams can steward resources in a relationally rich environment where there are ongoing checks and balances. When an organization loses its way and is no longer being faithful in its stewardship, it will continue to survive as long as it has resources. Families that train their children, on the other hand, have an ongoing source of new, Spirit-led direction. There are no foolproof plans. But God from the beginning of time placed the stewardship of His creation in the hands of a family instead of an organization, and He's still committed to stewardship through the family.

We are working with our kids to build in them a sense of stewardship. We're always looking for age-appropriate assets they can take care of and steward carefully while we watch to see how they treat the results. As a father, I would like nothing more than to give my children a large arsenal of Kingdom resources and believe there is no one in the world I trust more to be faithful than my kids.

In addition to working with kids individually as we build up their skills as stewards, the creation of a family foundation that allows the family to give as a team and that works alongside income-producing assets can help the whole family work together to prayerfully consider the investment of the King's resources.

We must talk to our kids about money early and often. They need to see how we make difficult financial decisions. The goal should be that when we die, nothing major changes. If you're already stewarding the resources together as a family and entrusting assets to your kids as they prove faithful, then your death should not create a huge, sudden distribution of resources that could throw the family into confusion or competition. Create the team culture as early as possible and pass the baton, if possible, while you're still alive and can give active feedback and support to your children so they can be great sons and daughters within their earthly families and, more importantly, faithful stewards of the resources of their heavenly family.

TOOL #7 - THE RHYTHMS OF THE FAMILY

Intentional rhythms help families find balance as they pursue a life of mission.

Living a Well-Ordered Family Life

"For God is not a God of disorder but of peace" -1 Corinthians 14:33

Everyone has some way of ordering their life. Some follow their heart and do whatever they feel at the moment while others fill up their calendars with the demands and expectations of others. But how should a family order its life? Does the Bible give us any direction to this crucial question? I was amazed to discover how much the Bible says about this subject... and equally amazed by how its clear insights are almost universally unknown by modern Christians.

The Bible gives families three extremely helpful tools that provide a way for developing an orderly lifestyle.

First, families have a clear leader or head who is responsible for this process and this person is called "the father" or "husband." This is extremely critical because there are powerful forces that will try and supplant the father from taking on and carrying out this responsibility. Forces outside the family like culture, demanding friends, bosses, governments, coaches, school systems, spiritual leaders and Madison Avenue will all attempt to wrest control of the family rhythm from the father in order to meet their own agendas.

Forces from within the family like the children or even the mother will often exert an alternate agenda. And finally, perhaps the most challenging force is the flesh within the man himself who will try and take control of the family to feed itself instead of what's in the best interest of the family and the family's mission. But no matter how weak, ill-equipped, passive or confused the father may feel, he is the only hope the family has at living a well-ordered life. God has designed him for this task. Men were designed to be strong-willed, persistent and vision-driven in order to provide both a shield against the encroaching agendas that want to control his family and to give the family its own capable, courageous leader. Men need to follow God's lead and be jealous for their own families. Men, if we don't provide clear direction and leadership to our family then there's a long line of others who will gladly take control for us. We cannot allow this to happen.

Second, as we discussed earlier, families are given identities through Scripture. These are in the form of our missions, our roles and who we are before God as slaves set free and adopted children in God's royal family. What do these things have to do with living a well-ordered life? Everything. Western people are notorious for making a common mistake when it comes to time management. We get caught up in action first, instead of beginning by asking "who are we?" This doing vs. being dilemma is a root cause of so many Western problems. We were designed to do out of who we are. If your doing does not flow out of your being then you will, by default, allow cultural forces to define who you are. Christian parents will allow a coach or a job or a pastor to define the family rhythm and before they know it, their entire rhythm is so jam-packed with activities they don't have any time left. And these families never even stopped to ask who they are. Doing has completely eclipsed being. But what if families developed a deep biblical understanding of who they are and then chose to express those identities through regular, family-directed activities?

That brings us to the third tool we have for living a well-ordered life and that tool is the rhythm. Way back in Genesis

1, God created a series of rhythms. "On the fourth day God said, "Let there be lights in the expanse of the heavens to separate the day from the night. And let them be for signs and for seasons, and for days and years (Genesis 1:14)." In addition to days, seasons, months and years fixed by the sun and moon, God gave us the week by creating the world in six days and resting on the seventh day. These rhythms create the canvas on which we order our life. These are not arbitrary periods of time, they are God-designed, and they are tools given to us to find ways of rhythmically expressing our identities.

So let's dive into how to do this practically beginning by looking at this tool we call "the week".

Living in Sevens

"The Sabbath was made for man, not man for the Sabbath..." - Jesus (Mark 2:27)

Why did God create the world in seven days? Why not in an instant? On Mount Sinai, God actually reveals to Moses the reason for the seven days of creation. He commands them to work for only six days and rest on the seventh day, "For in six days the LORD made the heavens and the earth, the sea, and all that is in them, but he rested on the seventh day. Therefore the LORD blessed the Sabbath day and made it holy (Exodus 20:11)." So this idea we call the "week" was founded in Creation and laid out as a pattern in the Ten Commandments and was further explained by Jesus as a gift given to mankind (Mark 2:27).

But like any gift, it must be received and used if we want to experience its blessing. So why did God give us the week? Western people think of these time periods very differently than most classical peoples. In the West we think in a very linear fashion. Life is a line that stretches out before us. We don't know exactly when it ends but we assume that point is a long way off. Life is extremely difficult to manage as a single line. For example, how much should you work if life is just a single line? Some people may become workaholics because they see work as a means of achieving a good life while others will try to avoid work and retire as early as possible. Living life on a line can also lead to deep depression if, for example, you expected to get married at 25 and you're now 30. When can you say you're living a truly "good life" or when that life has been irreparably ruined and should just be discarded?

Contrast that with viewing life primarily as a series of weeks. Instead of being given one long line that can be easily ruined by one major setback, think of life as a gift of thousands of weeks. The goal then becomes to learn to live a better and more balanced week. The picture is not a single line or an endless circle but a long spiral. This breaks down the task of ordering and living life into measurable and manageable segments. You can only be what you can do in seven days. So if I'm a father, husband, business-owner, tennis player, disciple-maker, son of the Father and writer then I must fit those identities into rhythmic weekly activities. This provides a meaningful boundary to who I am and what I can realistically achieve. If I'd also like to be a musician then I need to fit that identity into a week, but if seven days go by and I don't pick up my guitar then I'm really not a musician. I've abandoned that identity. If I want to properly steward my talents, relationships and opportunities, then I must faithfully fit them into a weekly rhythm. I'm not waiting around for that big break or that perfect person or graduation to start my life. I'm given a week right now and I need to live life this week and then find ways of improving my rhythm for next week.

This kind of rhythmic living is wonderful for family. Family relationships are clearly at the top of the list when crafting and improving our rhythms. Children also thrive in this kind of structure. We teach them from a young age how to craft and live a really good week. This is the essence of stewarding our time and energy faithfully.

Getting started living rhythmically is pretty simple. All you need to do is keep the Sabbath. Having a day of rest during your week will begin to force your life into a series of sevens. When we lived in Jerusalem it was pretty clear how the Sabbath not only implicates one day per week but forces every day to become special. Sabbath begins on Friday night so Thursday and Friday during the day are very busy preparation days for most families. When the Sabbath ends on sundown on Saturday, Saturday night becomes a fun time for hanging out with friends. Sunday launches the week and usually kicks off with an explosion of energy.

Rabbis have noticed that in the Exodus 20 version of the Sabbath commandment it says "remember the Sabbath" but in Deuteronomy 5 it says "observe the Sabbath." They picture that from Wednesday to Friday we look forward and prepare for the Sabbath, which goes along with the word "observe," while Sunday to Tuesday we "remember the Sabbath" and all that it means as it leaves its imprint on our lives heading into the next week.

Christians don't need to keep a sabbath day but I believe God designed us to live in sevens with a day of rest. Burnout typically comes from the monotony of every day being the same or the uncertainty of every day being totally different. We were designed for a balance and need just the right amount of sameness and change. This can be created by carefully crafting a weekly rhythm and continually reviewing and improving it.

Digging Deeper

- [Online Course] The Seven Day Family - Discover the single most powerful tool in history that brings life, order, fun and meaning into the life of the family.

If you are reading the physical copy of this book you can find the links to the digging deeper resources at familyteams.com/FR.

Crafting a Year

"For everything there is a season, and a time for every matter under heaven." -Ecclesiastes 3:1

Why do we have this concept called the "year"? Why is it 365 days long? What is its true significance in our lives? If you asked most people to describe their favorite traditions, they will most likely point to something that they do or experience annually. Christmas dinner at Grandma's house, the annual family vacation, or a trip taken with friends. A year is a very powerful rhythm. 365 days seems just the right amount of time when the memory of last year is distant but not forgotten. Re-experiencing a beautiful, annual tradition seems almost magical. Even people who typically resist traditions in general tend to relish annual traditions like everyone else. And children live for them. Their anticipation and explosive joy surrounding annual celebrations infects everyone around them.

So if these annual traditions are so deeply enjoyed why do so many of these events seem to be losing steam? In the west we don't understand the true purpose behind annual rhythms and so marketers have seized on this confusion to steer every annual event in a direction that will allow them to sell more products. But remember, God created the year and in the

Torah He teaches us much about its true purpose.

When God began to craft the culture of a nation, he spent more time helping them to craft a year then on almost anything else. The year is the ultimate tool in the creation of any culture because a year gives us the ideal length of time to tell an epic story about what really matters.

God designed the year as the rhythm where each core identity gets its own period of time. So on Yom Kippur (the Day of Atonement) Israel remembered their sinfulness and God's holiness, on Sukkot (the Festival of Tabernacles) they remembered that they are on a journey of faith and on Passover they celebrated God's redemption plan. The year is the canvas through which a family expresses and celebrates the most important things about who they believe God is, man is and what life is really all about.

If someone were to look at the traditions you repeatedly celebrated the past five years to determine who you are, what would they uncover? It's often said that if someone looks at your checkbook they can determine what is most important to you and in a very similar way someone should be able to look at your year and determine who you believe you are.

If you are like most westerners this is a fairly new concept to you. We, in the west, just let the culture tell us what, when and how to celebrate. This is a massive missed opportunity. If you want to found a strong, well-trained, multigenerational family, the annual rhythm is one the most critical tools in your arsenal. Let's learn to use it.

Begin by placing a blank annual calendar on the table and consider what you would like to celebrate on an annual basis that expresses who you are in Christ. When I began to do this, I chose to redeem holidays instead of inventing new ones.

Celebrations are far more powerful when they are done in community and when I began to understand God's purpose behind the annual rhythm I found the biblical holidays in the Torah to be perfectly balanced expressions of who we are and gave a common point of reference for our friends to join in.

All of these biblical holidays center on Jesus the Messiah. And even more than that, they tell us who we are as redeemed children of God. Most people know that the modern western calendar was primarily a Christianization of pagan holidays, but few know that the biblical holidays were actually outlawed by the Church for hundreds of years because they were labeled as Jewish in an atmosphere of rampant antisemitism. I personally don't have any problem with redeeming popular western holidays as Christian holy days to be celebrated in the home in a way that blesses the family. But I've found introducing biblical holidays into our annual rhythm as well has been surprisingly helpful in beginning to understand the real purpose of a holy day.

Biblical holidays can also help with balance. How do I know how many days I should focus on a subject like God's holiness and my sinfulness? God commanded the Jews to do this for a week, culminating in Yom Kippur. The Catholic calendar sets aside 40 days through Lent, culminating in Easter. Which is the right balance? Or should we just do both and add them together? We need to remember that when we focus on one subject we're also not focusing on other important identities. There are disadvantages to overcelebrating any single identity. I've found the Torah to provide a helpful baseline in discovering a balance of identities. God had an annual calendar in front of him and we have the results of his vision in the Torah. That is why I always recommend it as a helpful starting point for Jew and Gentile alike.

Paul insists that we never judge others for celebrating or for not celebrating certain holy days (Colossians 2:16). Remember, we have freedom in Christ. You can use your freedom to celebrate or not celebrate. You can invent holidays or recapture lost ones. But I really encourage you to craft an annual rhythm for your family. Strong families have strong identities and I know of nothing that strengthens identities more like fun, immersive, recurring annual holidays celebrated as a family.

TOOLS FOR LIVING A RHYTHMIC FAMILY LIFE

Family Meals

"Your children will be like vigorous young olive trees as they sit around your table" -Psalm 128:3

When you picture a healthy family enjoying one another's company, what scene comes to mind? A frequent picture across many cultures is a family sitting down to eat together. I believe there is something unique and special about the family meal that expresses, at some deep level, the essence of family. It's what we do when we want to experience our "familiness."

In western cultures, this typically becomes a discussion of how to spend more dinners together as a family. This is a great thing to work toward, but a family meal is more than enduring 30 minutes of polite conversation around a table.

In most cultures there are two kinds of family meals—formal and informal. When my wife and I got married, we were encouraged to register for two kinds of dishes, formal and informal. I had no idea why. We ended up receiving a whole set of china dishes from my wife's grandmother who scrimped and saved for many years to buy one piece at a time. But after receiving them we couldn't figure out exactly when to use them. This is one of many examples of our current culture living with a faint memory of an older, largely forgotten culture. We have the tools given to us to have two kinds of meals but we don't understand the purpose of either one.

I believe a formal family meal is crucial to the development of a multigenerational family team. Having a weekly formal meal where the family plays out the roles of father, mother, son and daughter (extended family included if possible) will give each member a deep sense of their place in the family structure. And, by the way, you get to define what "formal" means for your family. It doesn't need to have anything to do with what we traditionally think of as formalities (fancy clothes, nice dishes). But by "formal" I'm describing the whole family choosing to set aside a particular meal as special, prepare for that meal and experience a variety of elements during that meal.

These roles and parts can be tweaked for what fits your family and the gifts of each member, but as the meal progresses, everyone should feel like they fit comfortably into the larger family and have an important part to play. If someone is missing, then their absence should be felt during a formal meal. Will this feel awkward at first? Yes, it will. Do it anyway. As you make this time your own, that awkwardness will eventually give way to a sense that this is a natural, normal and essential element of your family's culture.

There is something deeply sacred about the family that our mocking and jaded culture does not understand, but this is the first step toward recapturing and experiencing that sacredness.

Informal meals are also very important. Having a formal meal takes some of the unnecessary pressure off of making informal meals too uptight. But this rhythm should also be crafted with some degree of care.

I was watching a documentary that described a night at Thomas Jefferson's house Monticello. After the meal each night the family, with their guests, would retire into the parlor to drink tea and spend 3-4 hours discussing things they learned or were pondering lately. Without the television or other individualistic electronic means of entertainment I think we'd still do this to avoid boredom.

When I first heard about this practice my first thought was, "Oh, that's what a family does." I grew up in an age where it was natural to entertain myself or go off with friends but it makes sense that, in the absence of these things, a family would need to learn to interact and really enjoy each other's company. So 3-4 times per week we have an informal meal followed by what we simply call "family time." This can be done around the dining room table or the coffee table but it's been an amazing experience. I begin by asking if anyone learned or had any ideas or questions they've been pondering about God. We move from that topic into a more general question like, "Did anyone learn anything today or have something they want to discuss?" We share stories from the day, passages of things we've read, watch funny videos or play a family game. At the end we often talk about what's in store for tomorrow and pray together.

Digging Deeper

- Shabbat Activation - We have chosen to use the Shabbat meal (Sabbath) as a starting point for the creation of a formal family meal. Here is a training and some resources on how we practice this rhythm.

If you are reading the physical copy of this book you can find the links to the digging deeper resources at familyteams.com/FR.

Holy Days

"Your children will ask you, "What are we celebrating?" And you will answer..." **-Exodus 12:26**

While spending a semester in Jerusalem I began my daily walk from the hostel where I lived to the college campus and was surprised to see these little huts had suddenly popped up everywhere. Every home had one in the front yard, every restaurant had one on their porch and even the hotels had them on their decks. I had no idea what in the world had happened. After living for 23 years in the US I began to experience, for the first time, a true holy day and it changed me.

This festival week is called Sukkot or the Festival of Tabernacles. God did not want the blessing of homes and land in the Promised Land to change the narrative of the way He expected the Israelites to live life. He wanted them to remember they are still not home but on a journey of faith. So every year a father builds a temporary dwelling outside the house, moves his family into it, and points back at the house to teach the children that this is not our real home. We, like our father Abraham before us, walk by faith. What Christian child, growing up in the affluent west doesn't need to learn that lesson?

Immersing the whole family in a multi-sensory experience of some essential biblical truth is how God designed the biblical holidays. In the west children perceive our holiday celebrations as more of a family fun day with, occasionally, some religious lesson woven in. Parents themselves often don't know or emphasize the spiritual meaning behind the holidays they lead their family to celebrate.

During a holy day, symbols are the essence of what connects it to its meaning. When children ask, "Why do we do this or that?" each answer causes them to understand at a deeper and deeper level the spiritual truth being celebrated. To have multiple competing meanings in one holy day gives our kids a kind of multiple choice of meanings and in the west, the secular meanings of our holidays are often portrayed with greater clarity. This ultimately results in the original meaning being lost.

In the Torah, the solution to the problem of just going through the motions was the father or patriarch. He presides over the holy day and ensures its meaning is understood. He answers the children's questions and initiates conversations about why we celebrate and gives the meaning behind each symbol.

Family teams must start, repeat and guard new or restored traditions that are full of meaning. It's a lot more work to restore a holy day or start a new one than to simply celebrate an old one. To avoid being completely overwhelmed, our family focuses on either starting or further developing one of these per year; the rest we repeat while trying to add small improvements. After many years of doing this we have a number of rich, restored, meaningful holy days we enjoy as a family. As we immerse ourselves in these annual traditions, our identity deepens in their meaning each year.

Digging Deeper

- [Audio] Equipping Families to Celebrate the Spring Holidays

- [Post] <u>Celebrating Sukkot</u> - Living Rhythmically Toward A Future: an explanation of why we meditate on eternity.

If you are reading the physical copy of this book you can find the links to the digging deeper resources at <u>familyteams.com/FR</u>.

Family Summits

"If any of your fellow Israelites fall into poverty and are forced to sell themselves to such a foreigner…They may be bought back by a brother, an uncle, or a cousin. In fact, anyone from the extended family may buy them back." **-Leviticus 25:48-49**

As family teams develop, and their efforts create wider spheres of influence, more entities and more members, then having an annual summit becomes critical. Today you're often considered to have a strong family if you consistently pull off an annual family reunion. While this kind of gathering is far better than nothing, why does a family need to reunite repeatedly? If your family functions like a team, you may be united in so many ways that a reunion is unnecessary, but what may be very necessary is an annual event where the family experiences its larger, collective familiness and prepares to work together to lead the family into the year ahead.

We've experimented with family summits and plan to do more of them in the future, especially now that our family is getting stronger and more diverse.

Family summits are a place to recast and reinvigorate the overall vision of the family team. Members should be reminded who they are and the unique calling or callings God has placed on the family. Patriarchs and matriarchs can refocus the family as a group to commit wholeheartedly to the service of God and his Kingdom.

Family summits are a great place for celebrating both the individual and collective accomplishments from the previous year. They are a great place for children and adults to demonstrate hard-won skills. Rites of passage of all kinds can be recognized and celebrated by the whole family.
A critical part of any summit is the crafting of tactical strategies that pull on the diverse skills of various family team members to accomplish the family mission. Various family members can give presentations of opportunities in which the family can invest and further develop together. In addition, family members can relate struggles they are having with developing their own callings, while others rally around them and provide valuable assistance. Imagine being an artist in a family that is committed to helping you fully realize your God-given gifts. Imagine if there are children with special needs where the resources of the family can come alongside and provide assistance. Many challenges, from sicknesses to widowhood to unemployment, may be too overwhelming for individual families but not for large, loving, coordinated extended families.

Family summits are also a place where relationships can be strengthened and love for one another can be expressed. Everyone who participates, from young children to great-grandparents, should feel highly valued and a part of something much bigger than themselves.

The open discussions, informal conversations, exciting presentations, displays of talent and exuberant celebrations at an annual family summit are the natural center piece to the year of a strong, growing family team.

Generational Rhythms

"Blessed are those who are invited to the wedding feast of the Lamb." - **Revelation 19:9**

The deeper the family identity becomes the more the family should consider ways of putting their own unique stamp on generational rhythms like births, funerals, weddings, baptisms, rites of passage, graduations and other once-in-a-lifetime events. Our culture has a certain understanding of what these events mean and how to recognize them but this understanding is unlikely to fully align with the convictions of a biblical, multigenerational family team. We must craft these celebrations in a way that deepens both our family identity and our understanding of the true meanings of these events.

Births are extremely important to the family, but in western culture, there isn't a very effective way of celebrating each child when they enter the family. Jewish families have a major celebration on the eighth day of the birth of a son at the time of his circumcision and God had some of his most faithful servants present at the celebration of the circumcision of his son. Simeon, for example, lifted the eight-year-old boy in his arms and rejoiced, prophetically foretelling significant elements of Jesus' life. How will your family celebrate the birth of new family members?

Funerals represent one of the greatest opportunities in the life of a family to reinforce the family vision and the overall meaning of family. The younger generation comes to this time of mourning with soft and open hearts to hear and understand how this family member gave their life for God's Kingdom and the various ways they worked to strengthen the family to better accomplish its mission. We shouldn't just blindly follow the burial and funeral rituals of our culture.

Consider creating, for your own family, a way to grieve, remember and celebrate the passing of family members that really builds the family up. This moment, more than any other, causes us to experience the reality that family is a multigenerational endeavor. Soon an entire generation will pass the baton to the next and the more we accept and work with the multigenerational nature of family life, the more successful this passage of resources, leadership and mission will be.

Weddings, to a multigenerational family, represent the creation of a new family alliance. While the couple is typically consumed in romantic love and the process of becoming one, something else very significant is happening on the sideline of the ceremony. Two separate families are linking arms. These families have a powerful incentive to help one another for the health of this new family being born on that day and those new relationships must be thoughtfully nurtured during the joyous time of celebrating this new marriage. Consider ways your family can bless and enfold the your new in-laws in a way that you both become much stronger as a result of your children's marriage.

Each once-in-a-lifetime event represents a great opportunity to strengthen the family team. Thoughtlessly celebrating these events in a way that simply mirrors current cultural trends can be wasting a once-in-a-lifetime opportunity to build up your family team. Before the pressure of these events comes upon you, consider crafting unique ways you can symbolize and celebrate what your family is all about.

Digging Deeper

- [Documentary] Betrothed - A documentary about how the Brayden and Talitha Waller celebrating their wedding by going back to biblical principles

about how Christ will one day come for his bride.

If you are reading the physical copy of this book you can find the links to the digging deeper resources at familyteams.com/FR.

CONCLU-SION: GOD'S KINGDOM AS A FAMILY OF FAMILIES

"For this reason I kneel before the Father, from whom every family in heaven and on earth derives its name." -Ephesians 3:14-15

God is a Father building a family. Throughout Scripture we can see that God longs to create a covenant people, but God's fathering heart comes out clearly and vividly in the New Covenant. His covenant people are not just a nation but his family. He wants to adopt us and give us to his Son as a bride forever. The mystery of why family exists has been revealed to us and all the family relationships we experience on Earth are merely a foretaste of what we will all one day experience when the Kingdom comes in its fullness.

That is why we must both preserve the true meaning of family and strengthen our own expressions of it. The people of God on the Earth today are a family of families. If people are going to recognize the healing and health brought by the Kingdom of God, then they must see a different kind of family than the one being expressed in the west.

I hope and pray this blueprint will help strengthen your family and that your family will grow to reflect the beauty of our collective family. Families transformed by the Gospel, living for the Kingdom and united with Christ and one another will begin to bring hope and point to the only true, lasting healing available for our fallen world.

Epilogue by April Pryor

February 5, 2019

I remember having the thought about 15 years ago or so, "It's all about the men!" I giggled at myself and told Jeremy, "It's all about the men! I love men!" Kind of a strange thing for a loyal wife to utter, but I had been thinking through society's problems, many of which I was relationally connected to in one form or another: teen pregnancy, homelessness, petty theft, high school dropouts, drug addiction, etc. I was mentally tracing those situations back to their source and it was slowly dawning on me that it was when the family of these people started falling apart, largely due to the dad taking off, that the course of these troubled souls had shifted, sometimes gradually, sometimes drastically, towards a slippery slope that could soon spiral out of control and therefore eventually negatively affect society at large.

At the time, Jeremy and I were knee-deep in the stage of young children and bounced back and forth from survival mode to thriving, largely dependant on where I was in the pregnancy/ recovery/ nursing/ potty-training cycle. It seemed like as soon as we had figured out a new rhythm that worked, or just gotten the next person to sleep through the night, something would shift and we'd be back onto the undulating waves of a growing family. The idea of being able to reach the men and fathers of the larger society rose and faded in and out of our conversations.

Some of you might be thinking, "What about the women,

wives, mothers?!" Don't get me wrong: we are awesome! We are super-important and have great worth and value and, let's be honest, the guys couldn't do it without us. But I do believe God's order of things puts the husband as the head of the family, and families are directly affected by whatever degree the father either rises to the challenge, becomes complacent, or caves in to all the pressures around and abandons his family and therefore the generations. The enemy hates God's order and has gone hard after the men, playing on the curse from the Fall in Genesis, and it has and is wrecking families, the very entity that God ordained to be fruitful and multiply and fill the earth. That's where we need to start: with the men, husbands, fathers.

If God the Father can capture the hearts of men and "turn the hearts of the fathers towards their children" (Malachi 4:5-6, Luke 1:17), it could turn the tide! How exciting is that?! I am the daughter of a man whose heart was captured by the Good Father, and as his relationship with Jesus grew, my dad's heart turned towards us kids and transformed our generational trajectory. You see, my grandpa's mentality was, "She wanted the kids, let her raise them." My grandpa didn't have much to do with the kids until he realized that my dad had some usefulness. As a 15-year-old boy, it became apparent that my dad had propensity towards mechanics as he started to repair motorcycles in their family-owned Triumph motorcycle shop. My dad's example of fatherhood was one of distance, dis-interest and conditional love. Any success my dad had growing up was largely due to my grandma, who was determined to give her kids every opportunity she didn't have growing up in the hills of southeastern Ohio.

My parents became believers after they had been married for a year through the ministry of the base chapel at Moffitt Field Naval Air Station in California in April of 1967. It started them on a journey of slowly becoming sold-out Christ followers and, as children entered the scene, it spilled over into how they should parent, shape their family and view the future of their family. My dad made career changes in favor of the family. He had impressed all the right people and was on track to move right up the chain in the Air Force back in the days when one computer took up a whole room and satellite control was cutting edge. He was given top secret assignments in the days of the Cuban Missile Crisis and was doing important work. He realized how this important work could take away from his family time and traded it out for a move back to Ohio and downgraded himself to civilian work at Wright Patterson Air Force Base. Continued insights from the Lord and growth in his faith and understanding of Scriptures continued to draw him closer to our family. He got ideas about how to raise us that felt revolutionary to him. The ideas of training his kids to obey his voice, to have an allowance to steward resources, to memorize Scripture, to do activities together as a family were all mind-blowing thoughts that excited him and gave him energy. He was interested in the four of us, had ideas of things to do for us, and made a move back home to where my parents were from so that we could be near both sets of grandparents. He had a plan of things he wanted to teach us that would be necessary for life (like changing brakes on a car!) and he took advantage of teachable moments.

And right there beside him as he made these discoveries, was his praying wife, my mom. She is a fully capable, quick-thinking, soft-hearted, early adopter and some of her spiritual growth might have been at a quicker pace than my dad's. As she saw his failings and bumblings, she was learning how not to criticize but rather encourage his attempts, how to control her desire to nag and instead let the Holy Spirit be the Convictor. She had grown up with a stronger sense of family and had to be patient as my dad made his discoveries. She changed her career from teaching in a school to being single-focused on creating an environment in the home that made it... well, home. She gave of herself and created a home in the truest sense of the word: a place of peace, order, fun ideas, being relaxed, having responsibility, serving others, and enjoying each other.

In March 2016, we had the privilege of celebrating my parents' 50th wedding anniversary in a weekend-long series of amazing events, the first of which was a dinner out with Mom and Dad and us four kids with our spouses at a private room at a nice restaurant. All 20 grandkids were babysitting themselves back at Grandma and Grandpa's house. We had a very nice dinner and went around the table in intentional conversation reflecting on Mom's and Dad's relationship and the different seasons they had lived through. We asked them questions, they told stories, it was a very sweet time. It was truly a picture of the good life we see in Psalm 128. As we were winding down, my dad suddenly stood up so suddenly he almost knocked his chair over. He got choked up and had a hard time getting his words out. He said, "I think I need to say something." He took a moment to collect himself.

"Some of you know, the Lord's put on my heart, 'What does blessing actually mean?' Jeremy has a midrash and one of the guys was talking about going into his baby son's room and giving him a blessing and all of a sudden he said, 'What have I just done?' What is a blessing? So, I've been kind of trying to decide what a blessing is. We had a couple of grandkids over and I asked them what they think a blessing is and they had a few good ideas. I've looked into it and you know, like the Beatitudes? Blessed is the man who does so and so and such and such. April sent me an email and it quoted Judges 1:15, about a girl coming up to a judge and asking for something and then asking for a blessing. And so I think this is the time that I should offer you all a blessing."

He choked up, had to pause for a minute, then continued. "You know, we don't know how long we're gonna be here. The Lord's given me a long life. I appreciate all of you and all the things you've done for us and for one another and I just want… if there is any power in God Almighty passed on to me that I can pass on a blessing to you, I do that. God bless all of you and may God lead you and guide you."

The room was quiet as we began to absorb what had just happened. His strength seemed to fade a bit and he just had to share, "So, I just thought, all of a sudden, I realized, all of you are here, so close, and this is a time, if ever there was, for me to say how much I appreciate you and how much of a blessing you've been to me, and I want to pass on that blessing to you."

Eight months later, he passed away suddenly of an aortic aneurysm.

As you reflect on what you have read in this book, may it be a tool that the Lord God Almighty can use to pass on blessing to you and the generations after you as your heart turns towards Him first and your family.

Made in the USA
Columbia, SC
09 March 2021